THE
People Manager's
Toolkit

A practical guide to getting the best from people

KAREN GATELY

JB JOSSEY-BASS™
A Wiley Brand

This book is dedicated to my parents, Denise Darwent and Paul Mitchell, whose love and belief in me have underpinned my success at every stage of my life. I love you both and I'm very proud to be your daughter.

First published in 2013 by Jossey-Bass

A Wiley imprint

www.josseybass.com

John Wiley & Sons Australia, Ltd

42 McDougall St, Milton Qld 4064

Office also in Melbourne

Typeset in 11/13.5 pt Bembo Std

© Ryan Gately Pty Ltd

The moral rights of the author have been asserted

National Library of Australia Cataloguing-in-Publication data:

Author:	Gately, Karen.
Title:	The people manager's toolkit: a practical guide to getting the best from people / Karen Gately
ISBN:	9781118590898 (pbk.)
Notes:	Includes index.
Subjects:	Management—Handbooks, manuals, etc.
	Leadership.
	Executive ability.
Dewey Number:	658.4092

Cover design by Paul McCarthy

Cover image © GETTY/Yuji Sakai

Author photo © Ikon Images—Ken Latrou

Printed in Singapore by C.O.S Printers Pte Ltd

10 9 8 7 6 5 4 3 2 1

Contents

Preface

Many years ago I found myself disillusioned by what I saw in the world of business. Everywhere I went I observed 'corporate carnage'; lifeless people simply going through the motions, turning up to work each day to endure yet another painful experience of earning a dollar. It was and remains common for me to observe unhappy people slogging through their work life with little or no passion for what they do. Just as common are those unfortunate souls whose wellbeing I have seen jeopardised by the consequences of poor leadership.

For a long time it has seemed obvious to me that when people are unhappy at work, everyone loses. This means not only the individuals themselves but also their employer, the people paying them and hoping they will realise their full potential in their work. Then there are the people around them, their colleagues and their family members, who are also more often than not affected by their attitudes, behaviours and state of wellbeing.

Standing at a crossroads in my work life, I felt I had two choices: I could retreat and follow an easier path removed from the nasty realities of business, or I could stay the course and find a way to make a difference. The spark of hope I felt at that time was fuelled by the people I had witnessed who were enriched by success and happiness at work. My own experience of loving my job and the people I worked with inspired me to want to help others to find that in their life. I recall thinking that surely if everyone was passionate about and deeply engaged with their work and organisation, the world would be better off for it. This belief underpinned the decision I made to work hard to influence the strength of the human spirit through great leadership in business.

This book, together with my first book, *The Corporate Dojo: Driving extraordinary results through spirited people*, are one part of my efforts to act on that decision. What drives me, however, isn't just a desire to positively influence the quality of people's lives. The many years I have spent working with people has convinced me that the human spirit is the key to achieving outstanding results—that is, results that generate not only more money for shareholders but also positive outcomes for communities and environments in which businesses operate. With more people with a strong spirit we will have more kindness, better decisions, and greater tolerance, forgiveness and understanding in the world.

Leveraging deep reserves of positive energy to drive business performance is unquestionably commercially smart. To me it seems logical that energised and capable people purposefully doing smart things really well will produce better results. My aim in *The People Manager's Toolkit* is to guide you towards achieving outstanding commercial results while at the same time making a positive difference to the lives of the people you lead, their families and the communities within which they live and work.

Happy reading!

Karen Gately
July 2013

About the author

Karen Gately is a passionate optimist with an unwavering belief in the power of the human spirit. A speaker, adviser and educator in the fields of human performance and leadership, Karen brings a fresh perspective to the art of being a successful manager. With her focus on leveraging both talent and energy, Karen shows leaders how to drive performance through inspiring, results-based leadership.

In this and her first book, *The Corporate Dojo*, Karen presents a compelling argument for why focusing on both results and people is critical to success. Karen does away with ambiguous concepts and arms leaders with realistic strategies and practical solutions. Her pragmatic, uncomplicated and down to earth approach sets her apart from many other commentators in her field.

Throughout her corporate leadership career, Karen has worked in client service, strategy and planning as well as quality-management roles. After eight years with The Vanguard Group, where she was the head of human resources for the Asia–Pacific region, Karen founded Ryan Gately, an HR consultancy based in Melbourne, Australia. Together with her team, Karen works with organisations large and small across a broad range of industries to support them in building and leveraging talented and energised teams.

Karen's approach is deeply rooted in the 25 years she spent training and teaching karate. At the age of 14, Karen was the youngest person to be awarded a 1st dan black belt in Shukokai karate. She then went on to be graded to 3rd dan after many more years of dedicated training and teaching. A multiple-time winner of state, national and international titles, Karen was also a highly accomplished tournament karate competitor.

Karen holds a Bachelor of Applied Science and Master of Business (Human Resource Management). She lives in Melbourne with her husband, Kevin and their three children — Jordan, Callan and Tamsyn.

Connect with Karen:

Website: www.karengately.com.au
Twitter: @karen_gately
Facebook: www.facebook.com/karengatelyAU
Blog: karengately.wordpress.com

Acknowledgements

This book would not have been possible without the love and support of my husband Kevin and our three beautiful children, Jordan, Callan and Tamsyn. Thanks Kev for everything you have done to look after our family while I have been locked away again in my writing 'bubble'. Thank you to each of you for encouraging and believing in me. You energise my spirit and enrich my life every day.

Thank you to my Ryan Gately team, Siobhan, Tom, Elaine and Taylah, for all of your hard work and support. Your belief in not only this book but everything we are doing together to influence the strength of the human spirit through business is greatly appreciated.

Thank you to Lucy Raymond, Elizabeth Whiley, Jem Bates and the rest of the fabulous team at Wiley. I am grateful for the opportunity to work with you and appreciate your contribution to creating a book I am very proud of. You have been a pleasure to work with.

To all of our clients, thank you for the opportunity to work with and learn from you. Each of the challenges and successes we have shared has contributed to what I have learned about people in business and how to leverage their full potential.

Last but certainly not least, thank you to each and every person who has encouraged my efforts and shown their support through their comments posted on my blog, Facebook and Twitter pages. It's difficult to describe the uplifting impact of your comments, especially during the very long hours I've spent writing this book.

Introduction

Never underestimate the power of dreams and the influence of the human spirit. We are all the same in this notion: The potential for greatness lives within each of us.

Wilma Rudolph, American Olympic gold medallist

Whether you are the CEO of a global organisation or a supervisor in a small business, your job is essentially to build and leverage a team capable of achieving outstanding results. While easy to say, this can be hard to achieve. Whether I'm working with small enterprises or large corporations, wherever I go I consistently observe the same challenges in managing and getting the best from people at work. Finding and recruiting the right people, tapping into their discretionary effort and influencing behaviours that enable success are examples of the complexities of people management I regularly encounter.

Even the most capable and experienced people manager is likely to encounter challenges leading their team. Many of those I work with struggle to keep up with the unrelenting demands of their role, and find their focus and time are consumed by dealing with people-related problems. It takes energy and discipline to effectively apply the strategies and approaches needed to meet these challenges, and commitment and strength of spirit to overcome the many obstacles you face.

While there are many inherent challenges in managing people, with the right attitude and approach exceptional standards of performance are possible. Each of the approaches and tools described in this book have the potential to increase your success in hiring great people, leveraging their talent and keeping them engaged with your business for the long term. However, there is no magic wand in the people manager's toolkit that can make predictable work of leading teams. Ultimately, the tools we will explore are valuable only to the extent that they are effectively applied.

Focused and disciplined application of these approaches and tools will enable you to:

- hire, develop and retain talented people

- motivate consistently high standards of performance

- inspire discretionary effort and loyalty

- support people to grow with your business

- overcome the challenges of poor performance and unacceptable conduct.

Before we explore the tools and approaches needed to drive success, we will first consider why both human capabilities and spirit matter. In other words, why are influencing the knowledge, skills and experience but also the depth of positive energy people bring to their work critically important priorities for every people manager?

The importance of capable people behaving successfully

Great results are achieved when capable, highly engaged people invest energy and behave in ways that enable success. There is no doubt that success depends equally on capabilities and behaviour. When talented people are motivated to bring the full strength of their knowledge, skills and experience to their role, truly great outcomes are possible. A manager's ability to develop the talents and capabilities of their team and to influence successful behaviours drives the level of performance that is ultimately achieved.

To illustrate this point, reflect for a moment on how often you have observed or worked with the kind of person I refer to as the 'incompetent genius'. These individuals are unquestionably brilliant, with deep knowledge, skills and experience, but they fail to perform because they struggle to work effectively with other people. Now think about another common kind of person: they are enthusiastic and work hard but they also fail to deliver because they simply don't have the abilities needed to get the job done. Finally, reflect on people you know or have observed who bring together both the behaviours and the talents needed, and as a consequence achieve great results.

Understanding team spirit

I firmly believe that all human beings have access to extraordinary energies and powers. Judging from accounts of mystical experience, heightened creativity, or exceptional performance by athletes and artists, we harbor a greater life than we know.

Jean Houston

Imagine for a moment your team's spirit as a ball filled with positive energy. The more energy contained within the ball the stronger your team's spirit. The spirit of each member of your team determines the energy they have in reserve and can unleash in pursuit of their objectives. The vitality, enthusiasm and drive each person brings to their work is drawn from this reserve of positive energy. It is also from this energy source that people draw strength to keep striving through challenging times.

Every people manager plays a critical role in influencing the strength of their team's spirit, individual by individual and as a team. Their primary focus must be on pumping positive energy into the team's spirit and doing everything possible to limit those things that have a draining effect. Negative energy doesn't dilute our spirit; rather, it has the effect of depleting our positive energy. How often have you experienced the draining effect of a negative person's company? If we are feeling strongly energised, their influence may be only marginal; if we are already drained, however, these individuals can quickly diminish our vitality. Even when we are highly energised, over time such people can drain the life force from us.

Workplace influencers of spirit

Each person is unique, and to influence their spirit requires an understanding of what makes them tick. Here is a brief summary of the five most common influencers of the human spirit at work.

1 Personal value

Our sense of personal value reflects how we feel about ourselves as well as how we believe others feel about us. Positive emotions we should encourage include:

- how I feel about me: valuable, qualified, capable and successful

- how I believe others feel about me: valued, trusted, respected and accepted.

2 Relationships

The quality of our relationships at work can influence our spirit. Whether with our boss, colleagues or staff, or with clients or service providers, what we feel from other people and what we feel towards them matters. The types of positive emotions we want people to feel include:

- what I feel from others: appreciated, supported and safe

- what I feel towards others: trust, respect and regard.

3 Purpose and meaning

The extent to which we are able to find purpose and meaning in our work also plays a role in energising or draining us. How we feel about what we and our organisation contribute matters. Doing a job that has an altruistic purpose energises many people, while for others purpose and meaning derive from the harmony between their values and those of the organisation they work for. Still other people want to feel a part of something bigger than themselves or to contribute to the organisation's success. Examples of the types of positive emotions we want people to feel include:

- what I feel from what I and my organisation do: satisfied, fulfilled and rewarded

- how I feel about what I and my organisation do: proud, ambitious and passionate.

4 Belief

The strength of our belief is reflected in how we feel about the future and our ability to influence that future. For many people, belief is a vital source of strength and resilience. Examples of the types of positive emotions we want people to feel include:

- how I feel about the future: hopeful, optimistic and encouraged

- how I feel about my ability to influence the future: confident, empowered and certain.

5 Enjoyment

Liking what we do matters. All too often I meet people who are fundamentally unhappy in their work. If we don't like our job or enjoy doing it, it is unlikely to energise us and will likely drain our spirit. Examples of the types of positive emotions we want people to feel include being entertained, interested and amused doing what they do.

The relationship between spirit, behaviour and performance

The strength of a person's spirit influences the behavioural choices they make. Whether consciously or otherwise, each person on your team chooses the behaviours they bring to any given situation. A strong spirit enables people to make positive choices even if at that moment they don't feel particularly happy about their situation. Those with plenty of positive energy in reserve are better able to choose effective ways of behaving. If their spirit is weak or drained of positive energy, however, the same feelings may lead to poor choices of behaviour.

When they feel capable, trusted, respected, accepted, included, appreciated or empowered, the vast majority of people enjoy an energised spirit. Energised people are far more likely to behave in ways that enable success, such as being driven, courageous, honest and committed. Equally, when people feel betrayed, disregarded, insecure, bored, worried or confused, their positive energy is likely to become drained. When that happens they are likely to behave in ways that diminish success. For example, they may become withdrawn, resistant, lethargic, hesitant, pessimistic and even destructive.

Central to a people manager's role is influencing their team's spirit and, in turn, the behavioural choices they make. Among many important reasons for focusing on the strength of your team's spirit is the value of tapping into their discretionary effort—that is, what they do because they want to, because they have emotional ownership of the results. Tapping into the energy people are willing to invest when they are passionate can yield superior performance. The managers who are able to leverage this passion are those most likely to lead the way, to break new ground and to achieve long-term success through their team.

The people manager's toolkit

Successful leaders not only approach their role in ways that inspire people to follow; they effectively leverage the tools available to them to build the strength of the human capabilities and spirit needed to drive results. Included in every people manager's toolkit are the essential systems, processes, policies, programs and resources that underpin an effective approach to human resource management. In some organisations specialist expertise is also provided through services delivered by HR staff and external suppliers. When close working partnerships are formed, this expertise influences people management strategy and practices, and therefore success.

Across the diverse range of industries I work with, regardless of the organisation's staff numbers, turnover, profit, growth, prospects or stage of development, when it comes to managing people the same principles always apply. These core ingredients of success are the focus of the chapters ahead. There are lots of books written about each of the topics we will explore, great books that provide deep insight into particular theories, models or experiences. In this book I will focus on the things that matter most as fundamental priorities for every people manager.

Included in *The People Manager's Toolkit* are strategies and practices focused on:

- vision and strategy

- culture management

- recruitment

- communication

- performance management

- learning and development

- reward and recognition

- change management

- HR services.

These essential tools, and how to leverage them effectively in your organisation, provide the framework for this book. Our focus throughout is on how to apply each tool to build the capability of your team and to nurture the strength of their spirit. First, in chapter 1, we explore the foundations of a successful approach — the ways in which every manager of people must behave in order to earn the trust and respect needed to inspire people to follow their leadership. We look at the key characteristics of the approach to managing people that is most likely to get the best from them.

Next we explore in depth each of the tools in the people manager's toolkit. The first priorities we look at, in chapter 2, are creating an inspiring vision for the future and mapping the road to success. We reflect on why confronting your current reality with honesty matters and the most important things you must do to get every member of your team on board and playing their part. Proactively building confidence in your team's ability to succeed together and an accurate perception of what it will take to get there are fundamental to the approach advocated.

From there we explore how to create and manage the culture of your team or business. We look at how to identify the behaviours you need from every member of your team and the core values these reflect. Central to the focus of chapter 3 are the priorities you must set and the actions you must take to embed your organisation's values in the way people behave. As an effective people manager you will not only espouse your core values but proactively operate in line with them to create a healthy, vibrant and successful workplace culture.

In chapter 4 we look at how to find and recruit the right people when you need them. We explore how to develop pools of talent you can tap into from within and outside of your current team. Fundamental questions to reflect on and discuss with others when assessing the suitability of each candidate include: How well is she suited to the role you are looking to fill? What is the likelihood that he will cope with the inherent challenges of the position? Are they likely to bring culturally aligned values and behaviours? We explore in detail approaches to planning and implementation that will ensure that each candidate hired fits with both the capabilities and behaviours needed.

Communication is an important enabler of all successful relationships and teams. In chapter 5 we examine the most important ingredients of effective communication. We explore productive approaches to communication that ensure the right people are informed or consulted at the right time in the most effective ways. We look at the two-way nature of good communication and how best to balance telling, asking, listening, questioning and challenging.

Chapter 6 focuses on how to leverage your performance management efforts for best results. We look at how to set clear expectations and enable performance through productive feedback. We also look at the crucial coaching role a manager plays and how to hold people accountable for achieving acceptable standards. This chapter guides you to inspire and lead people to achieve standards of performance that reflect their full potential.

In chapter 7 we look at how to grow the capabilities of your team through targeted learning solutions. We examine how to identify the right development needs and the initiatives most likely to add real and lasting value. This chapter investigates the approaches most likely to enable and realise development objectives including training, coaching and on-the-job learning experiences.

Rewarding and recognising people for the contributions they make and the standards they achieve are critical to your ability to inspire commitment and drive performance. Chapter 8 focuses on how to demonstrate appreciation both for the things people achieve and for the ways they go about it. We look at rewarding the right behaviours and outcomes as well as approaches to maximising the positive impact and benefits of these efforts for the individual and the team.

Guiding teams through periods of transformational change is a common concern for people managers. In chapter 9 we look at the core competencies for leading change and the important role of your ability to build and maintain trust throughout. Driving change well demands that you understand its impacts, assign clear roles and responsibilities, and engage stakeholders every step of the way. We look at these priorities and the influence of team culture on your ability to achieve ambitious and sustainable change objectives.

The final chapter of *The People Manager's Toolkit* is dedicated to the role of human resources and how the partnership between managers and HR professionals influences an organisation's success. We reflect on the characteristics of a successful approach to HR while taking an honest look at the common reasons many organisations struggle to realise benefits from HR services. We identify the most important capabilities you should look for in HR people and key indicators of performance you should consider when determining the value of HR services available to you and other people managers in your business.

As we work through each of the chapters, the extent to which these tools combine and influence one another will become increasingly evident. The manager's approach and the tools they apply form a web of interacting factors that collectively influence the spirit, capability and ultimately performance of the team. For example, your hiring decisions can create challenges or strengths in the areas of performance management, learning and development, and culture management. How you manage performance reflects and influences the culture of your organisation. The culture you create will influence your approach to rewarding and recognising your team. How you reward and recognise people will be reflected in your approach to performance management and learning practices. And so it goes on—every tool in your toolkit needs to be leveraged as part of a greater whole that ultimately leads to team success.

How to use this book

This book is intended to be a practical reference guide that points you to the things that matter most when it comes to getting the best from people at work. If you are an inexperienced people manager just setting out, follow the step-by-step instructions and utilise the checklists provided. If you are more experienced, apply the frameworks and success measures offered to appraise your current approach and effectiveness. Use them to regularly audit what you currently do and identify ways you can keep improving. If you are a manager of managers or an HR professional, leverage the pragmatic and uncomplicated guidance provided to grow the people management capabilities of others and ensure a consistent approach across your business.

Included in the 'What success looks like' section of each chapter are key performance indicators (KPIs). These reflect the most significant measures of successful application of each tool. Leverage these KPIs to continually monitor and measure the effectiveness of your people management efforts. In some cases performance standards can be quantified, while in others measurement is based on observation and qualitative assessments of the extent to which each tool supports you to meet relevant people management objectives.

Each chapter sets out key priorities that individually and collectively define a successful approach. While there is no 'one size fits all' solution, more often than not each of these priorities is important to successful application of the tool in question. Consider these priorities and be honest with yourself about how well you typically focus on and apply each when you need to. Remember, each tool will add value only to the extent to which you apply it well.

Also included at various points throughout this book are checklists designed to provide you with specific guidelines relating to the topic in question. Again, carefully consider each point and its relevance to what you are working to achieve. Each chapter concludes with a checklist summarising the absolute priorities that will enable successful application of each tool discussed, together with a summary of the most common mistakes or obstacles to success I have observed that you would be wise to avoid.

Each chapter includes a story about people and organisations I have worked with. Names have been changed to preserve the confidentiality of the people whose stories I have shared. These case studies illustrate real-world applications of the approaches discussed. Reflect on each story and consider any lessons that could be applied to your own approach and circumstances. Consider the actions that enabled success in each case and reflect on how they may be applied in your team or business.

This book describes approaches and priorities relevant to all people managers, but it is important that you focus on the specific objectives you are working to achieve and on what will add the most value to your business. While broadly applying the guidelines, you will need to adapt your approach to suit your unique circumstances or objectives. As you work through the book, note the aspects of people management that you need to place greater focus on, change or improve. If you are a manager of managers, reflect also on their development needs. Leverage what you learn by taking the steps necessary to enable you or the managers who work for you to develop in these areas. A flexible yet structured approach will allow you to apply the lessons that will add the most value and achieve the best possible outcomes.

In summary, use this book to establish approaches, monitor their effectiveness, and continually improve and grow your approach to managing and getting the best from every member of your team. Ultimately the key to getting maximum value from this book is putting what you learn into practice!

Chapter 1

People management—
the foundations of success

I believe the real difference between success and failure in a corporation can be very often traced to the question of how well the organization brings out the great energies and talents of its people.

Thomas J. Watson Jr, former CEO of IBM and
author of *A Business and Its Beliefs* (1963)

Your ability to influence the success of your team is driven by both your approach and how effectively you apply the tools in the people manager's toolkit. In later chapters we will look at how each tool can be applied to leverage maximum return on your investment of time, energy and resources. First, however, we will explore the approaches to managing people that enable us to exert a meaningful influence on their success at work. We will look at why personal ownership, accountability and leading by example matter as much as they do, and what a manager must do to foster healthy working relationships.

I will share with you why the same core values and behaviours influence the success of every manager responsible for a team, no matter what their level of seniority or how technically complex their department is. In this chapter we will look at:

- a code of management conduct that defines successful behaviours

- golden rules of engagement that underpin successful work relationships

- the importance of adopting an integrated approach that balances a focus on results and on people.

What success looks like

The primary indicator of the effectiveness of your approach to managing people is the performance of your team or business. Other measures of success are reflected in the capabilities, typical behaviours and effectiveness of the people who work for you. The most important indicators of successful people management practices include the following:

- High-potential candidates want to work with you and your organisation.

- Every member of your team is able to perform their role up to or above the standard expected.

- Most of the people on your team are proactively developing their capabilities and careers.

- You are able to access capabilities and resource capacity when needed.

- Behaviours are always aligned with business values and contribute to a successful culture.

- All staff feel they are treated fairly and have a positive perception of your business culture.

- People-related issues or challenges cause minimal disruptions or adverse impacts.

- Levels of staff turnover, both voluntary and involuntary, are generally low.

- People on your team choose to stay for longer than your industry average.

Case study
Quietly connected

Joe, the leader of a finance team for a large industrial manufacturing business, is one of the most capable and successful people managers I have ever worked with. Far from being the type of person eager to stand out from the crowd, Joe can best be described as a quiet achiever. Despite his reserved manner, Joe exerts a powerful influence on the engagement and success of his team. The rapid rate at which he has turned around their performance is strong evidence of the effectiveness of his approach.

Joe was hired following the abrupt departure of his predecessor, Malcolm, who had been with the business for more than 20 years, 10 of those in the role of finance manager. Joe's brief was to dramatically improve how the team functioned and what they achieved. In particular, the organisation was anxious to ensure that better governance and controls were established to mitigate the risks of non-compliance and errors. When Joe arrived, his team were buried in a backlog of work, struggling to get on top of things, let alone put improved systems or controls in place.

Joe addressed these issues and achieved the specific objectives asked of him very quickly. Over the months that followed he also took steps to ensure his team supported business decisions more effectively. Previously operating purely as a processing unit, under

Joe's leadership the finance team developed a trusted adviser relationship with the rest of the organisation. Experienced members of the team now work closely with business leaders and provide the financial data and analysis needed to support critical business decisions, such as those relating to tenders and acquisitions.

The first thing Joe did when he joined the business was spend time listening to and learning from both his team and other colleagues in the organisation. Over the first couple of months he worked hard to form a clear view of what was working well and what needed to change. Included in his assessment were the capabilities and spirit of his team and what was needed to enable them not only to meet the expectations of the organisation but to realise their full potential.

While some experienced managers would have been tempted to dive straight into solutions mode, Joe chose first to listen, observe and learn. He wanted to understand the role of each member of his team—what they were there to do, the obstacles and challenges standing in their way, and how they felt their own problems could be solved. Adopting a hands-on approach, Joe plunged into the trenches with his team and spent the early stages of his employment working alongside his staff.

It was impressive to watch the ways in which Joe engaged with his team and inspired them to achieve more. Not long after taking on the role, Joe had managed to win the support he needed not only from his staff but also from his peers. Now facing little resistance, Joe quickly established strong relationships that reflected the trust and respect he had earned. It was evident to any observer that Joe was clearly focused on the goals he was there to achieve and understood well the importance of his team in making that possible.

Many of the leadership qualities, priorities and behaviours Joe brought to his role are the subject of the remainder of this chapter. Outlined are the approaches needed by any manager looking to leverage the full potential of their team to achieve the best possible outcome.

A code of management conduct

While we can and should bring our own unique style and methods to the way we lead people, in this section I will share what any manager needs to do to effectively influence the success of their team. These are the non-negotiable foundations of a successful approach that will enable you to inspire and lead your team not only to reach their objectives but to far exceed them. We will explore the importance of and best approaches to the following:

- earning trust and respect
- assuming ownership and accountability
- leading by example
- collaborating and consulting
- building strong relationships
- balancing your focus between results and people.

Priority 1: earn trust and respect

Earning trust and respect is a prerequisite, a starting point from which to positively influence the thoughts, feelings, behaviours and ultimately performance of those we lead. It's important to remember that our ability to influence the success of others is proportionate to the extent to which they are willing to let us. Therefore to elicit best efforts, to push people beyond their self-perceived limits, to motivate them to move forward or to step up and have a go at things outside their experience, we need their trust and respect.

Trust and respect are equally important prerequisites to delivering tough love with positive effect. To be sure that the person on the receiving end of our constructive feedback will at the very least be willing to listen, we must have their confidence. If they are willing to listen they are more likely to hear, and if they are able to hear they are more likely to invest the energy or courage needed to respond usefully to our feedback. People are far more likely to be enabled and encouraged — that is, motivated to be courageous — by a leader they trust and respect.

Just as important as a team's confidence in their manager is the respect and trust the manager has in the team. Having faith in the character and competence of the people we work with allows us to delegate roles and responsibilities without hesitation or misgiving. While our trust must be earned, each of us as a manager also has a role to play in being open and receptive to trusting. This is easier said than done for some managers, but unless we are willing to be open to trusting others we will never reap the full benefit of our working relationships. An important influencer of your ability to trust is your willingness to respect what other people offer. Of course it is necessary to identify and address gaps in your team's capabilities, but it is also important to recognise and respect what they bring.

Lead with integrity

The integrity you bring to your role as people manager is reflected in the way you choose to speak to, guide and respond to members of your team. Equally, the decisions you make and the actions you take reflect the integrity you bring. Leading with integrity takes self-awareness and consciously choosing to apply high ethical standards. The form integrity takes will vary from one person to the next. Each of us will find its meaning reflected in our personal values and beliefs, and in our own understanding of how to live an honourable life.

Each of us must decide what integrity means. Here are some examples of the approaches typically adopted by successful leaders:

- Lead by example and demonstrate the standard of behaviour you expect from others.
- Be honest while maintaining sensitivity.
- Keep promises; honour what you say you will do.
- Make fair and reasonable decisions.
- Sincerely work in the best interests of the team and organisation.

Demonstrate humility

People are more likely to choose to follow you if they perceive you to be able to lead them confidently and with strength. Your self-belief will encourage the confidence people have in you, but this faith will soon be eroded if you are seen as arrogant or egotistical. Behaving in ways that reflect a sense of superiority or inflated self-perception will quickly undermine trust and cause hesitation, if not outright resistance, among those you ask to follow you.

Your capacity to acknowledge your imperfections candidly will influence the perceptions people have of your openness to learning. Listening to alternative points of view and being open to changing your position on any given topic are examples of learning to demonstrate humility and are critical to earning trust and respect.

To lead with humility, ensure you demonstrate the following:

- a balanced self-perception of your strengths and what you need to learn

- an openness to learning from others, including members of your team

- a recognition that you don't have all of the answers and are willing to listen to others

- acknowledgement and ownership of your mistakes.

Be authentic

Being genuine is essential. Despite all the advice in this book and in other books about how to become an effective manager, it remains important that you allow people to see who you really are. Being real, presenting an authentic version of yourself, is vital to your ability to earn and maintain trust in any relationship. No-one can lead effectively by trying to imitate someone else or being something they simply are not. Most people find it difficult to trust a manager who fails to demonstrate sincerity, so while it's important to learn from the experiences of others, trying too hard to be like them won't work. Authentic leaders never lose sight of who they are, and they demonstrate their values consistently.

To adopt an authentic approach, make sure you do the following:

- strive to be the best possible version of yourself, not someone else

- are sincere in your dealings with every member of your team

- let people get to know you

- are upfront and transparent.

Priority 2: assume ownership and accountability

Being a successful manager of people starts with taking ownership of your role. A half-hearted approach isn't enough; success takes a full and sincere commitment to leading your team. The depth of the ownership you feel is reflected in your intrinsic drive to assume responsibility for your job. Taking ownership is not something anyone else can make you do; you need to want to prioritise and invest energy in leading and getting the best from your team.

While some managers take seriously their responsibility to proactively drive the performance of their team, all too often focus is limited to their own individual contributions. It's astounding how often I meet managers who find the people management aspects of their role a distraction and even an irritation. Many of them are impatient at having to engage in activities such as one-on-one time with their staff, well-planned and -considered team meetings, and providing the direct guidance people need.

My question to these leaders is, if the purpose of being a manager is to manage, how can you achieve success without investing in the focus, time and energy required? No doubt a team can achieve a base level of competence and moderate success under a mainly self-focused leader. Great results, however, demand commitment and hard work from the boss. Taking ownership and holding yourself accountable for managing your team are the foundations of your success.

Priority 3: lead by example

Influencing passionate engagement and strong performance requires you to adopt an approach that causes people to want to follow you. It isn't possible to be a great people manager unless the members of your team believe in your approach and choose to comply with your instructions or abide by your wishes. Trust and respect are non-negotiable prerequisites to having this influence, and leading by example is core to earning and maintaining that trust and respect.

A manager's actions and words communicate volumes to people and rarely go unnoticed. Everything you do or don't do, say or don't say, influences people's perceptions of you. People typically observe their manager closely and judge the extent to which they should be trusted, respected and emulated. While a manager's fairness, consistency and integrity are crucial, people are also more likely to follow the example of an authentic, committed and generous leader.

There are many great reasons to lead by example, but the two most important are to:

- earn the trust and respect needed to inspire others to follow you

- enable the success of other people by positively influencing their behaviour.

Our ability to influence the way other people behave is drastically undermined when we fail to lead by example and practise what we preach. Few people trust or respect the kind of boss who fails to live up to at least the standard he expects from his staff. Robert, a manager I once worked with, expected people to own up to their mistakes but was quick to blame someone or something else when things for which he was responsible went awry. Unsurprisingly few people respected Robert's approach or trusted his actions.

Some people managers complain that it's difficult to maintain a consistent good example, especially when things are challenging or stressful. I appreciate the truth of this. Being a great manager, however, takes the strength of character to always do the right thing at the right time for the right reason. When next you find yourself without the strength to be a positive example, look for a way to avoid negatively impacting your team. Find your own circuit breaker that will help you manage the way you conduct yourself and the example you set not only for your team but for every person you work with.

Priority 4: collaborate and consult

To consult means to ask for advice or seek information from someone. Collaborating, on the other hand, means working with them to complete a task or achieve a shared objective. The vast majority of people I have worked with or observed in business respond well to a manager who both consults and collaborates with them and their colleagues. Managers who demonstrate respect for their staff, their point of view and their ability to contribute are far more likely to earn buy-in and inspire commitment.

As we will explore further in later chapters, actively tapping into the ideas of your team and enabling people to contribute to decision making are fundamental to your success as a people manager. Trust in your competence and character can be greatly strengthened if you work closely with your team. Communicating both frequently and openly, sharing your thinking, asking others what they think and how they feel, all profoundly influence your ability to get the best from people.

The most important things you should do when consulting and collaborating with your team are to:

☑ ask people to contribute ideas about what you should do and how you should go about it

☑ test your ideas, whenever possible, by talking to people about what you are thinking and planning

---

☑ remember that it doesn't all have to be down to you, so allow some decisions to be made by members of your team

☑ work closely not only with your team but with your colleagues across the whole business.

Priority 5: follow the 10 golden rules of successful relationships

Over the years I have been fortunate to have had the opportunity to work with leaders and teams across many different industries, in small and large organisations, in a variety of environments, and tackling a myriad of opportunities and challenges. No matter where and under what circumstances we meet, regardless of the conditions under which my clients are working, I consistently hear the same things about what matters most in building strong relationships, healthy workplace cultures and successful teams.

In this section I will share the 10 golden rules of behaviour that most people at work expect from one another. It is a manager's role not only to lead by example and to demonstrate these behaviours, but to encourage and enable them in others. As you reflect on these 10 rules of successful relationships, think about the role of each in building trust and respect.

Rule 1: value relationships

Before you can begin to influence the success of relationships you need to value and place priority on them. Unless you understand the importance of relationships to the success of your team and business, you are unlikely to play the role you need to. Too many managers ignore obvious signs of conflict or dysfunction and fail to influence the ability of people to work well together. Every people manager has a responsibility to nourish and enrich not only their own work relationships but also those among other people on their team and between their own and other departments.

While some managers adopt the view that it is not their job to get involved in stresses or conflicts that arise among their staff, without harmony and a spirit of cooperation performance will undoubtedly suffer. Work relationships influence not only how people feel about being there but also the extent to which they are willing to collaborate. Put simply, unless people work effectively and harmoniously with their colleagues, their spirit is likely to be drained and the collective potential of their team cannot be leveraged.

Rule 2: have and project a healthy attitude

None of us is perfect, and most of us are capable of projecting attitudes that don't always serve us well, but the strength of our relationships depends on our ability to bring healthy approaches to the way we interact with our colleagues. To build trust and respect among the people we work with, it's crucial that we don't convey a sense of being judgemental, sarcastic or cynical, or of mocking the contributions of others. Loading comments with attitude is likely to get most people's backs up, as is dismissing or trivialising the concerns they express. Demonstrating an aggressive or defensive attitude does little for the harmony or effectiveness of relationships and teams.

The best people managers perceive themselves as no better or more important than any other member of their team. They understand they simply play a specialist role focused on leveraging the spirit and capability of the team to drive results. This philosophy demands an absence of ego or sense of superiority. It takes determination and sincere desire to coach other people to succeed. These managers project a respectful attitude that strengthens trust and deepens respect.

Rule 3: be polite and courteous

Conducting ourselves with courtesy is crucial to building relationships based on trust and respect. There are endless examples of the types of behaviours to be modelled. Here are just a few I have often observed—both the benefits when they are done well and the consequences when they are not:

- Think before you speak. Choose your words carefully and deliberately to avoid inadvertently causing offence.

- Keep your mouth shut when you should. Be careful not to disclose or discuss sensitive information inappropriately.

- Speak civilly. Never bark orders or demands at people.

- Say please. It's a popular word, and while people may not always notice when it's used, they often notice when it isn't.

- Don't ignore people. Respond when you are asked a question; if you don't have the answer let them know that. This is important not only when we are communicating face to face but, in our increasingly technological world, in emails and online forums too.

- Say good morning. The way we greet one another, or don't as the case may be, can set the tone of our relationship for the rest of the day. Most people take it as a sign of respect if you invest the little time and effort it takes to greet them when you first see them. If you work with a large team it isn't necessary or always practical to do the rounds and greet every person. But walking in each day with your eyes to the ground or generally avoiding making eye contact is likely to be noticed and have a negative impact on how people feel about interacting with you.

- Say thank you. We don't need to make a big song and dance about everything people do, and showing appreciation certainly doesn't need to cost money. A simple thank you can go a long way to making people feel relevant and appreciated. It's important not to save our thanks for just the big moments; the day-to-day effort people put in also deserves credit. Yes, people are paid to do their jobs, but saying thank you can make a big difference to their sense of feeling valued. A simple thank you can inspire people to dig deeper and give more than a compliant contribution.

Rule 4: be compassionate and sensitive

People want to feel that the person they work for cares about them and their development. Most also want to know that their colleagues are cared for. Kindness and compassion are words used in the context of business far more regularly now than in the past. More and more people are recognising the importance of behaviours such as being considerate or thoughtful, caring about impacts and consequences for people, and even understanding and appreciating challenges people face outside of work.

Demonstrating compassion and sensitivity for the feelings and needs of others can have a profound impact on their spirit and your ability to influence their growth and development. Failing to be kind undermines the confidence people have in our ability to be fair and reasonable, sending a clear message that we are self-absorbed and incapable of balancing our own perspective with those of others. For some people, believing that we are heartless is enough for them to avoid engaging with us altogether.

To demonstrate compassion and sensitivity make sure you:

☑ show you care about the impacts of your decisions and actions on other people. This doesn't mean don't act; just care when there are consequences for other people, and do whatever you can reasonably be expected to do to support them through it.

> ☑ listen and demonstrate empathy. You don't have to agree with people or pander to their emotions, but most people need to know you are at least willing to hear them.
>
> ☑ reserve judgement. Don't dismiss people's feelings without first giving those feelings reasonable consideration.
>
> ☑ don't lose confidence in people just because they've had an emotional but very human moment.

Rule 5: be honest

Honesty means truthfulness and straightforwardness, the absence of lying, cheating or deliberately deceiving. Being upfront with people, and sharing as much insight as possible, always positions you more strongly for close and healthy working relationships. With this closeness comes the opportunity to positively influence how people behave and perform. Of course there are times when confidentiality and sensitivity demand discretion, reserved disclosure or closed doors, but I encourage you to consider how often that is really necessary. Always distinguish between appropriately withholding information and presenting a false truth. Being honest isn't about telling all, it's about sharing what you are able to and not suggesting things that are false and misleading.

More often than not, when faced with the challenge of not knowing how to respond, your best option is to say so. Most reasonable people understand you are not able to tell them everything they would like to know. Being honest about the fact is more likely to have a positive impact on your relationships than otherwise. At times anxious people eager to know more about events or circumstances may find it difficult to hear that you are either unwilling or unable to disclose information. But never underestimate the potential for harm in prematurely or inappropriately sharing insight into confidential or sensitive matters.

Rule 6: be visible and connected

Often I hear people complain about their boss or colleagues being aloof, remote or just hard to get to know. Most people want and expect to have access to the people they need to work with, including their manager. Equally, most people are uncomfortable when they feel deliberately excluded. Given the importance of visibility and transparency to the strength of relationships, it's amazing how many people managers choose to hide themselves away behind closed doors, walk through the halls with their heads down and ignore their staff in the lift or kitchen. Relationships can be especially undermined when people perceive an individual to be deliberately avoiding connecting and working with other members of the team.

Rule 7: acknowledge mistakes and shortcomings

Too often I see people vigorously defending their position despite having been clearly proven to be wrong. At times it is evident these people realise they are wrong yet still they persist. Most of us are capable at times of continuing an argument that has already been lost in order to save face or avoid accountability. It is important to the health of our relationships, however, to know when to back off and acknowledge we are wrong. When we deny our mistakes, fail to operate with an open spirit or refuse to shift our perspective in the face of compelling evidence, both trust and respect are eroded. The good news is that when we do acknowledge we are wrong or messed up, most people will give us credit, and we earn both trust and respect through our honesty.

Rule 8: listen to learn and understand

As we will explore in greater depth in chapter 5, communication is critical and most effective when it's a two-way street. While it's important to share information, the health of any relationship depends equally on people feeling they are heard. Most people are capable of listening to hear the information imparted but fewer are skilled at listening to understand. People don't always clearly express their perspective and certainly don't share everything on their mind. Listening deeply allows us to ask more questions and explore further the other person's point of view. Even if you disagree and ultimately don't do what people hope you will, they are more likely to accept the outcome if they feel their views have been heard, understood and considered.

Rule 9: be fair and consistent

Consistency is key. Unpredictable and seemingly inequitable behaviour can inspire people to be cautious and hesitant to trust you. If there are differences in the way you respond to similar circumstances, it's important that you explain why. It is critical that you are consistent from day to day, hour to hour, moment to moment, because being erratic throws people off and puts them on edge. Just as important is your ability to apply uniform and justifiable criteria to the way you go about making decisions that affect others. Make sure there are clear and reasonable motives behind your actions and decisions, or inevitably people will grow suspicious and distrustful of you.

Rule 10: leave ego at the door

Our confidence and sense of self-worth are deeply empowering aspects of our selves and are what often stands between our capabilities and their effective application. Like self-respect, a healthy self-regard is a powerful source of positive energy that fuels our spirit. Both self-respect and our ability to love ourselves have a profound impact on our happiness and, ultimately, on our success, not just at work but in all areas of our lives.

When our sense of self-worth is balanced by self-awareness and an understanding of how we can grow and improve, we maintain a healthy ego that has a positive influence on our approach and achievements. When we allow ourselves to develop an inflated view of our own importance, rightness and capabilities is when we are likely to stop learning from and collaborating with our staff and colleagues. Ego is not entirely a bad thing but it does need to be kept in its place, and sometimes that's at the office door.

Priority 6: adopt an integrated approach

It is common to observe leaders operating at one end or the other of a spectrum of leadership approaches. At one end of this spectrum is the manager focused on achieving results; at the other is the manager focused on the needs and wants of people. Results-focused leaders commonly adopt an intellectual approach, while the approach of their people-focused counterparts is typically characterised by empathy. Put simply, intellectual leaders ('results guys') follow their head, while empathetic leaders ('nice guys') follow their heart. Both bring strengths to a business; equally, both are capable of shortcomings that undermine their ability to successfully leverage the full potential of their teams.

Great leaders adopt an integrated approach that combines the strengths of both a results and a people focus. It is an approach characterised by a dedicated focus on achieving optimal outcomes while also engaging the passion and energy of people. Integrated leaders are driven and ambitious, but their understanding of the importance of leveraging the spirit and capabilities of people to make outcomes happen has a strong influence on their priorities and actions.

While I have met and worked with many managers who bring an approach consistent with that of an integrated leader, when the pressure is on many of them will reveal a tendency towards behaviours consistent with one end of the spectrum or the other. To understand what it takes to be an integrated leader, first we will explore in greater depth the polarised characteristics of results- and then people-focused leaders.

The 'results guy': an intellectual approach to managing

The intellectual leader is considered smart, but is often neither liked nor respected. There is rarely doubt in anyone's mind that they are in charge; they never hesitate to lead and typically drive hard to get the job done. Clearly focused on achieving results, the intellectual leader's weakness is in their ability to engage with and leverage the full potential of people. Common enabling and diminishing characteristics of an intellectual leader are included in table 1.1.

Table 1.1: enabling and diminishing characteristics of intellectual leaders

Enabling characteristics	Diminishing characteristics
Results focused with a strong desire to get the job done	Shows little regard for how people feel
	Fails to consult with others
Disciplined and structured	Disregards the views of others
Analytical and logical	Closed and makes isolated decisions
Measures outcomes and holds people accountable	Holds unrealistic expectations
	Fails to listen
Command and control	Inspires conflict
Applies process to manage quality	Rigid and uncompromising
Provides direction and instruction	
Takes corrective action when needed	

The 'nice guy': an empathetic approach to managing

At the opposite pole of leadership approaches is the empathetic leader, the 'nice guy'. These are the leaders who collaborate widely and bring people together in pursuit of a common goal. Empathetic leaders are often known for their emotional ownership of results and their unwavering commitment to the relationships they form. Their well-developed ability to make people feel heard and valued means their teams typically believe they contribute to important decisions, including priorities set and directions taken. Common enabling and diminishing characteristics of an empathetic leader are shown in table 1.2 (overleaf).

Table 1.2: enabling and diminishing characteristics of empathetic leaders

Enabling characteristics	Diminishing characteristics
People focused	Pander to emotion
Value relationships	Avoid conflict
Empathetic and care for others	Leave issues unresolved
Intuitive and creative	Hesitate to make decisions
Persuade and influence	Hold unrealistic ideals
Flexible and adaptive	Fail to ground ideas
Easygoing	Frequently change priorities and direction
Discuss ideas, solutions and approaches	Inappropriately share insights or information

An integrated approach

By integrating the polarised leadership approaches of the intellectual and the empathetic leader, we maintain the strengths and begin to overcome the weaknesses inherent in each. The integrated leader places equal priority on the need to achieve results and to engage people effectively in the process. Balanced in their thinking, they are typically commercially astute and understand the link between people performance and business results.

With a balanced focus on results and people, integrated leaders drive and inspire; they command and influence. Central to their effectiveness is their ability to lead by example and to earn trust. Respected by their staff, peers and other leaders, managers who adopt an integrated approach generate and unleash positive energy in others and leverage discretionary effort.

Integrated leaders are able to:

- provide a clear and inspiring vision of the future

- articulate the plans for turning vision into reality

- achieve outcomes with discipline and rigor

- hold people accountable with conviction and fairness
- face and share reality truthfully and compassionately
- inspire others to strive to achieve their own and shared objectives
- achieve outcomes through the capabilities and spirit of people
- engage authentically and encourage a genuine approach from others.

When we integrate the typical characteristics and approaches of the intellectual and empathetic leader, the 'middle way' becomes clear. Table 1.3 illustrates where this integrated path to effective leadership lies.

Table 1.3: the integrated path to effective leadership

	Results guy	Integrated leader	Nice guy
Primary focus	Achieving the outcome	Leveraging people to achieve result	People; needs and wants
Priority	Care for the business	Balanced care for all	Care for staff
Style	Professional formality	Authentic leadership	Familiar informality
Expectations	Challenging demands	Realistic ambition	Easygoing preferences
Accountability approach	Tough and direct	Tough love	Lenient and elusive
Decision making	Logic	Values-driven logic	Beliefs
Interpersonal engagement	Emotional detachment	Compassion	Empathy
Communication	Reserved	Deliberate and targeted	Unrestrained
Empowerment	Strict boundaries	Guiding principles	Free will

Chapter summary: the most important things to do and avoid

Must-do checklist

The fundamental priorities of any people management role include the following:

✓ remember your job is to manage people, so make your team your number one priority

✓ own your job and invest the time and energy it takes to be an effective manager

✓ be honest with yourself about how committed you really are to driving great results through people

✓ see yourself as neither above nor more important than anyone else on your team

✓ lead by example and be the best possible example of the approach you want from others

✓ share accountability for success with each member of your team

✓ be compassionate, and show it

✓ learn from and teach everyone around you.

Common mistakes to avoid

The most common mistakes I observe people managers make that grossly undermine their effectiveness are:

✗ being the type of manager people are intimidated by or are uncomfortable being around

✗ failing to love all their kids equally (favouritism doesn't serve a leader well in any environment)

✘ lying to their team (people will see straight through you, and you will lose their trust and respect; if you can't tell them, say so and why)

✘ staying in their office and failing to work closely with their team (it's the only way to understand and leverage their full potential).

Chapter 2

Vision and strategy

You have to dream before your dreams can come true.

Abdul Kalam, former President of India

Defining and leveraging a clear vision and strategy are important leadership priorities that enable you to direct, inspire and engage your team. In this chapter we will explore how providing a clear view of where you are heading and why, the plans in place to get you there, what you need from each person and when it's needed, underpins success. We will look at how to motivate people to engage with your vision and passionately execute your strategy, and outline what you must do to ensure every member of your team understands the role they are expected to play and is determined to succeed. We will look at how to:

- dream big and yet ground your ideas in reality
- understand your current reality and what needs to happen to achieve your vision
- lay out a clear plan to achieve your strategic objectives
- link company vision and strategy with the role of every member of your team
- engage your team in the process and encourage ownership of plans for the future.

A clear vision achieved through intelligent strategy executed well is the model approach to driving business or team performance. While simple to say, applying this approach in reality can be challenging. Sometimes the most significant obstacles to success are those that arise along the way, such as lack of information, resistance and pushback from people, systems issues, budget constraints, and issues relating to customer expectations and stakeholder support. Changing circumstances, shifting priorities and unanticipated events can turn our plans on their head, requiring that we start again or dramatically change tack. The clarity of your vision or the relevance of your strategy can shift quickly, demanding a considered and agile response from you and your team.

While maintaining a clear vision and targeted strategy every step of the way can be challenging, in many organisations I have observed the real problem is a lack of clarity to begin with. Many of the teams we work with have only a vague notion of what they hope for from the future. While they know they want to deliver quality products or services, continue to grow their client base or revenue, and perhaps even implement new systems or processes, they lack the targeted plans to make this happen. Often their focus is limited to traditional pillars of business performance such as client service, process quality, financial management and sales. While these teams do adjust their approach if needed, their unplanned response is often slow and at times misguided.

Frequently I meet business owners or CEOs who have a clear picture in their own mind of what the future holds. Occasionally their teams are vaguely aware of these dreams, but what is often missing is a strategic plan to turn these dreams into reality. 'I plan to grow the business and sell it in five years' or 'to achieve the growth targets agreed and then move on to my next challenge' are typical ambitions. The quantum of the intended growth and time horizon involved can vary greatly, but the overall objective is the same—drive growth and then get out. When you ask these leaders how they intend to make that happen, most point back to the pillars of business management. Fewer speak of targeted strategies, the capabilities that will underpin their success or the team members responsible for particular initiatives or aspects of the strategy.

Whether you lead a large or a small team, a whole organisation or a division, own your business or are employed as a manager, adopting a planned and considered approach to achieving your vision and strategy is crucial to success. Your vision lays out your intended destination, your destination guides your strategy and your strategy determines action. It's taking the right action that leads to success. Without a clear view of the destination it can be near to impossible or, at best, hit and miss to choose the right actions to take. Teams that lack a clear vision and strategy are more likely to respond to the unexpected with a knee-jerk reaction and to lose sight of priorities as they scramble to tackle new challenges.

What success looks like

The most important measures of how successfully vision and strategy are leveraged include the extent to which there is clarity across your team and how engaged people are. Important indicators include the following:

- People understand what the organisation is trying to achieve and the role their team plays.

- Each person understands their own role in enabling the success of their team and the business.

- Key strategic objectives and important priorities are understood and given focus.

- The organisation's vision and strategy are translated into plans for each team.

- People regularly challenge plans for the future and intended approaches.

- Vision and strategic plans reflect realistic ambition; they are achievable but demand stretch.

- Progress is monitored and measured.

- A focused yet agile approach is adopted.

- Honest reflection and acceptance of reality underpins the approach taken.

Case study
Focused agility

The technology industry moves and changes at a rate that would make many business leaders' heads spin. A product that is at one moment 'hot property' can in the next be superseded and rendered obsolete by something better, faster, cheaper and often smaller. Exciting ideas that one day are at the leading edge can the next day be running at the back of the pack. To innovate in this fast-paced world takes agility and the ability to move more quickly than your competitors, both those you already know and those who are beavering away in their parents' garage on the cusp of creating the greatest technological breakthrough the world has ever seen.

Working with a mid-size technology firm gave me a ringside view of what is possible when an organisation adopts a dynamic and evolving approach to the vision and strategy of their business. For Geoff, the CEO of this firm, the notion of an annual business planning process was laughable. As he explained it, if Geoff and his leadership team waited a year to decide what they would do next they would most likely be out of business before that day arrived. Working with them over time it became clear that every member of this leadership team considered it their responsibility to continually question and challenge what they were working to achieve and how they were going about it.

This organisation is among the few I have observed that chose to change tack and head in a new direction part way through the execution of what had until then been considered an important initiative. The launch of a competitor's solution demanded they find a way to differentiate their approach. This meant going back to the drawing board and challenging all their previous thinking. Not only did they find a new and better way forward, but their solution very quickly became a leader in its field. This was not a cue for Geoff and his team to take their foot off the pedal. It was extraordinary to watch the extent to which they shifted gears from celebrating their win to planning their next move.

The most important thing Geoff did as CEO to enable this agility was to make the process of dreaming about the future a necessary and ongoing part of the way every leader and indeed every team member was expected to approach their role. Geoff expected managers to lead by example and in turn dedicated time every week in his senior management meeting to innovation and exploring the implications of industry trends or events for their vision and strategy.

The influence of the approach taken by Geoff and his leadership team was clearly evident across the business. Weekly staff meetings encouraged and applauded ideas and feedback from their team about what was working or not working so well. Nothing was considered sacred; everything was up for debate. Every member of the team was viewed as a valuable source of insight into not only what was already happening out in the market but also what could and should be done. This is an organisation that is unafraid to challenge and shift its approach even if that means moving in a radically different direction.

While the overarching vision of the business shifted little in the time I worked with them, their strategy was far more dynamic. The goals and priorities that enabled their vision ultimately to become reality shifted. Mostly these shifts were marginal, but twice in two years I saw them dump major initiatives to shift focus to more important strategic priorities. Among the most dynamic businesses I have observed, they continue to grow and prosper, leading their industry with innovative solutions created from the imaginations of their team.

Adopting a strategic approach

Most days I work with managers who plug away with good intentions, doing their best to achieve vaguely defined objectives and standards of performance. Some management teams rarely come together to talk about plans for the future and how the organisation is positioned to make them happen. A lot of managers fail to bring their teams together to talk about what they must achieve over time and how they will go about it. I regularly meet people who struggle to align the vision and strategy of their team or organisation with the role they personally must play. This lack of clarity is a significant stumbling block to adopting a strategic approach to people management. Getting the best from people must start with ensuring they are aware of your vision and strategy, and intimately understand what they can and must do to support success.

Vision and strategy are unquestionably important tools in your people management toolkit. They are tools that provide clarity, set direction, establish priority, focus efforts and channel contributions from every member of your team. Your vision and strategy not only enable you to purposefully and deliberately build your team's capabilities; leveraged well they can be a powerful tool in your efforts to inspire commitment. In the following sections we will explore how to create your vision, the importance of fully and honestly confronting the reality of your current circumstances, and putting the plans in place to take you from where you are now to where you want to be. We will also look at the importance of inspiring engagement in your vision and strategy and how to win the buy-in of each member of your team.

Dream the dream — creating an inspiring vision of the future

The starting point of any successful endeavour is understanding and articulating the outcomes you want to achieve. However, the hectic pace at which so many managers and teams operate often makes achieving this clarity and focus difficult. With our minds occupied with here-and-now priorities there is often little energy and space created for reflecting on future possibilities. In this section we will look at the things that matter most to enabling you to create and continually evolve your vision. Before we do, however, it is important to understand what we mean by *vision*.

Vision is a picture of your company or team in the future; it's your inspiration but also the framework for your strategic planning. Vision isn't limited to the 'big picture' view of the organisation's ambitions; the vision each team has of their own future matters just as much. Every team must understand how they contribute to turning the organisation's vision into reality. Vision is also important to the projects or major initiatives in which organisations invest vast sums of money and resources. Whether applied to all or only part of an organisation, a vision statement should answer the questions, 'Where do we want to go?' and 'What do we want to achieve?'

Priority 1: keep dreaming

Visioning is neither a one-off nor a once-a-year event. Looking into the future, dreaming about what may be possible and imagining the places where you would like to go are crucial if a business or team are to achieve their full potential. Our ability to continually grow and evolve depends on curiosity and the desire to keep exploring new and better things to do. The great entrepreneurs of our time have shown the importance of innovating, adapting and responding to a changing world. Richard Branson, Steve Jobs, Oprah Winfrey, Bill Gates and Walt Disney are celebrated examples of what a visionary leader is able to create and keep creating day after day, year after year, decade after decade.

The process of creating your vision is something that should be ongoing. Constantly evolving your vision to align with the world in which you operate is critical to your ability to remain relevant and progressive. Having a vision statement that clearly articulates your view of the future is important, but so too is a cultural environment that allows people to feel safe, and be inspired, to challenge your vision at any time. Only by adopting a flexible and responsive approach to creating your vision will you achieve sustainability and growth in an ever-evolving and changing world.

Priority 2: dream big and believe in possibilities

No-one in life achieves big things by believing in small possibilities, or so I believe. While this idea has been central to my thinking for many years, I can't recall where I first learned it. Over the years I have witnessed endless examples of the direct correlation between what people achieve and the extent to which they believed they could. As Henry Ford famously said, 'Whether you think you can, or you think you can't —you're right'.

Every leader I have observed achieve amazing results through their teams has done so by first creating an inspiring vision of the future that people believed in. Without exception these managers have been capable of winning buy-in by encouraging belief in exciting possibilities and in the team's ability to succeed. These managers not only influence their team's confidence that big things can happen but also inspire in them a passionate desire to strive to get there.

To achieve the best possible outcomes it's critical that you and your team challenge conventional wisdom. Limiting your dreaming to within the boundaries of what is commonly understood or accepted is likely to lead to ordinary results. Being a leader in any industry takes a willingness and ability to think beyond convention—to have the courage to take the road less travelled, or even one that has never been travelled at all. Our history is rich with examples of the achievements of people who dared to think differently and give new things a go.

By promoting a creative culture you are more likely to continue to expand your own vision and realm of possibilities over time, and it is these expanded possibilities that will empower you and your team to reach the highest peaks of your potential. Your own ability to conceive of a bigger and brighter future matters, but so too does your ability to inspire that belief in others. For most people, however, achieving everything they are capable of requires them to challenge their unfounded or limiting beliefs.

Many of us have fears and beliefs that influence the choices we make about how to behave, which ultimately hold us back. For example, if we perceive something as a threat or constraint, it can influence our decision not to act; we may hesitate or turn away at the very time when our best approach is to move forward and confront the challenge head on. Influencing people to choose courage, determination and resilience in the face of their fears often takes encouragement and coaching support.

Priority 3: have realistic ambition

Your vision must be ambitious if you want people to reach for new heights; however, it is also essential that your team believe this vision to be realistic and attainable. An extravagant, unrealistic vision is likely to be met with general scepticism or disbelief. Asking people to set their sights on reaching goals they consider well out of reach can also lead to fear—fear of failure and of being held accountable for failing to achieve lofty ambitions. Others may simply not bother trying to achieve the expectations of a manager who demands they strive to achieve the impossible.

An important quality of the integrated leader, realistic ambition is the ability to hold high hopes for the future while having our plans grounded in an accurate perception of reality. Realistic ambition means your team believe your vision is possible and are motivated to dig deep to make it happen. Dreams that are within your reach, but only when every member of the team brings their best, are those most likely to encourage people to strive to achieve great things. Ambitious dreams that really make a difference to your business, industry, community or world are those most likely to inspire.

As we will explore later in this chapter, creating your vision with your team is the surest way to earn their buy-in. Remember, your vision is simply a tool you leverage to create an outcome—to focus your strategy and the capabilities and spirit of your team on achieving clear objectives. Providing your team with the opportunity to participate in the creation of this vision is a powerful way of ensuring they intimately understand its message and purpose.

Priority 4: ground your dreams

While allowing our minds to explore the far reaches of what is possible, it's important that ultimately we ground our vision in reality. People managers who successfully lead their team to achieve their vision are focused and clear about what they are working to achieve and what it will take to get there. The objective of creating a vision for your business or team isn't to convey the full depth and breadth of possibilities but to focus every team member on your core objectives.

Once you have an ambitious yet realistic vision of how your business or team will look in the future, the next step is to work out what needs to be done to make it happen:

- What time frame will you be working to?

- What resources will you need?

- What skills, knowledge and experience will your team need to achieve your vision?

Each of these questions must be answered through the strategic plan you create to guide your team along the journey. In the following sections we will explore the importance of facing your current reality, defining the priorities and identifying the steps you need to take.

Face reality

Armed with a clear vision of the future you want to create, next you need to understand your current reality—that is, your current circumstances, including the strengths you can leverage, the weaknesses you need to overcome and any obstacles that may stand in your way. Assessing your current reality equips you to understand what you need to achieve to move from where you are today to where you want to be.

Priority 1: tap into the insights of other people

One of the more common mistakes I observe managers make is to assess their current reality with little to no input from other people. While you are likely to have some accurate insight into what is working well and what needs to improve, never underestimate how little you may actually know. A multitude of things happen every day in your team that you are unaware of. In fact, there are likely to be lots of very important things you know absolutely nothing about.

As a manager you should expect that some people will try to manage your perceptions and in doing so cloud your view of the full picture. Keep in mind also that at times we can be so close to something that we look past the details staring us in the face. Take the time to ask your team what they observe. Ask other people, both within your organisation and outside it, for their views. Colleagues in other departments, customers and service providers, for example, can provide valuable insights into your current reality.

Much like creating your vision, assessing your current reality is something you should do on an ongoing basis. Being agile in responding to shifting priorities and new challenges requires that you maintain your awareness of reality at any given time. To achieve great results we can never afford to assume all is progressing as intended. Regularly tapping into the insights of your team and other stakeholders is an important way of keeping your finger on the pulse so you can respond as needed.

Priority 2: make it safe to tell the truth

Not everyone has the courage to volunteer information about things that aren't going well. The extent to which some people are willing to put their hand up and own to their mistakes, proactively draw attention to things that are going wrong or even suggest another way of doing something will depend on the trust they feel—trust that their feedback will be both welcomed and valued; trust that there won't be any adverse consequences for themselves or others if they share their views honestly.

Before you can reasonably expect people to share their perceptions and opinions, particularly about things they believe need to improve, you must create a safe environment in which that can happen. One organisation I worked with asked their team for feedback and then took action against some they accused of adopting a negative attitude that undermined the group's morale. Unsurprisingly the next time they asked for feedback few people were willing to participate. These types of behaviours from managers are fatal for trust and will undermine your ability to tap into what your team can offer.

Priority 3: understand the good, the bad and the ugly

Achieving your vision requires that you be armed with a complete picture of your current circumstances. As confronting as some people and teams may find it, you need to honestly appraise how things really are. Of course, while exploring reality it is always important to be respectful and sensitive towards the people involved. However, avoiding social discomfort should never hold you back from determining what isn't working, what is missing or what could go wrong if you take certain paths.

Many of the managers I have worked with over the years have been programmed to look for the things that aren't working as well as they should. They acknowledge the strengths to a limited extent, but they struggle to focus on the positives because of an ingrained tendency to look past what is working to what isn't. As you look down the path towards the vision you want to achieve, however, understanding the positives you already have to work with is an important priority.

Observing and understanding the value and potential of your current strengths matters every bit as much to your success as knowing what you need to improve. The strengths you have already built are both assets that can be leveraged and foundations upon which you can develop your capabilities further. Identifying, growing, maintaining and exploiting strengths should all be central to your strategic planning process.

Reflect on the strengths and weaknesses of your business as they relate not only to the people you have on the team but also to the maturity of other organisational capabilities such as your systems or processes. Just as important is for you to have an accurate view of the quality of and demand for both your products and services. Armed with an intimate understanding of your current reality, you can begin to lay down your roadmap to success.

Map the road

With a clear view of your destination and of where you are right now, you can begin to work out the detail that will enable you to put theory into practice—that is, how you intend to travel from point A to point B, the approaches and actions to be employed to turn your vision into reality. What path will you go down? What risks or obstacles might you encounter? What tactics will you deploy? What resources will you need and how will you apply them? These are just a few of the important questions you must answer to establish a well-considered strategic plan to guide your team to a successful outcome.

Priority 1: understand risks and obstacles

The effectiveness of the strategy and tactics you apply will in part reflect the extent to which they adequately account for and respond to obstacles or challenges that may arise. Choosing the best approaches requires you to contemplate and anticipate difficulties that may lay ahead. While the scope of this chapter doesn't allow for a full assessment of the types of risks and obstacles you should consider, examples include:

- team challenges such as key staff leaving, low engagement or a lack of capabilities needed

- competitor actions such as launching or changing products and services

- regulatory change such as substantial shifts in legislation or compliance obligations

- financial challenges such as cost blowouts or withdrawal of funding.

Allow your mind to sift through all of the circumstances that could derail your efforts. Contemplate from what direction you might experience an attack or counteraction, and from whom you could encounter objection or resistance. The possibilities may seem endless, but it's important that when formulating your strategy you focus on the obstacles and risks that are foreseeable and require serious consideration.

Identifying obstacles to your vision is not about finding reasons or excuses not to pursue it. Your goal should be to understand what your strategy must overcome to be executed effectively. Examining obstacles realistically allows you to craft innovative strategies to overcome them. In an ideal world you will avoid all potential roadblocks, but in reality that is not always possible. Sometimes the best you can do is to make your team aware of what may arise and identify ways you could respond.

Priority 2: choose your strategy

As with most things in life, there is usually more than one way to reach a destination. Now you know what you want to achieve, are intimately aware of your current position, and understand the risk and obstacles that can present, it's time to decide which path you will take. At times it is appropriate to leverage more than one avenue to achieve your vision. What matters is that you identify the specific strategies you will deploy to create success.

Focus on the core strategic objectives that will enable your vision — that is, the most important things your team need to prioritise and achieve to create the outcome you want. Typically it is useful to focus on no more than half a dozen core strategic objectives. For example, an organisation with a vision to establish a position as the leading provider in a new and still rapidly evolving industry may choose to focus on their team's capabilities and spirit, the product, service innovation and speed to market. Reflect on what approaches are most likely to enable you to win the race to reach your destination.

Priority 3: identify resources

Before you set out, make sure you know what resources you are likely to need along the way. Put simply, a resource is a source or supply from which benefit is derived. Your plans are likely to adapt to or shift with circumstances, but to get off to a good start and maintain progress you must have at your disposal the physical and human resources you need when you need them. Effective resource planning requires that you explore both the capacity and the capabilities you need for success. Consider which of these you already have access to, and which you need to build or acquire.

Important questions to ask include the following:

- What human capabilities (knowledge, skills and experience) will we need and when?

- How many 'staff hours' of effort is each initiative likely to take?

- How much excess capacity will allow us to be responsive while still being cost effective?

- What information and systems will be needed?

- What equipment or machinery will we need?

- What materials and supplies will reaching our destination most likely consume?

It would be reasonable to ask at this point why you do not determine your resources ahead of deciding on an effective strategy. Some managers believe the only way to develop a realistic strategy is to start with what is available to them. While that is true to some extent, until you have a sense of how you want to approach an objective it's difficult to know specifically what resources you will need and whether or not you already have them. With a clear view of your strategy you can predict with some accuracy your resource requirements. Your ability to leverage or collect the necessary resources may lead to certain tactical decisions.

Priority 4: decide on your tactics

At the next level of detail are the tactical manoeuvres you will engage — the specific initiatives or projects needed to execute your strategy. Tactics are the means by which your strategy is carried out; they answer the question, 'Who's going to do what by when?' This can be a challenging step in the planning process for many visionary leaders who find thinking about, let alone documenting and communicating, detail both tedious and frustrating. Remembering, however, that all the dreaming in the world will make little difference if we don't take action should help even the most creative person ground their ideas and develop actionable plans.

Priority 5: decide what you will monitor and measure

Reaching your destination will require that you monitor progress of the initiatives designed to take you there. Responding with agility to ensure you land where you intended to means you must understand your position at any given point along the way so you can identify any tactical shift you need to make. Establishing milestones—measures that indicate your progress—is a critically important although often missed or underutilised step in any planning process. Identify measures that will tell you:

- whether you are progressing on time and budget

- how critical processes, projects, systems or people
are performing.

Not only do you need to decide the things you will measure, but you also need to understand how you will measure them. Important questions you need to answer include the following:

- How will you capture or access the data you need?

- What resources, both human and otherwise, will you need to make that data capture possible?

- How much time and money will measurement take and can you see a reasonable return on your investment?

- What is the risk versus return ratio of implementing systems to enable you to measure and monitor your progress?

- What forums of communication need to be in place to aid your ability to measure and monitor? For example, what reports or meetings need to be produced or convened?

Priority 6: document your plans well

Simply documenting your plan isn't enough to ensure it adds value. Many strategic plans fail to add value because, while comprehensive, they are also overly complex or verbose. These documents are so overwhelming that once they are created they are rarely referred to again. Typically the problem lies not in the validity of the content but in the complexity and sheer volume of the information captured, making it challenging to articulate or digest.

These are the strategic plans lying at the bottom of desk drawers or filing cabinets in offices everywhere. Plans add value only if they are used; some of the ways you can ensure your document is referenced and easily applied include using:

- PowerPoint instead of Word (you are more likely to use fewer words and more pictures)

- checklists or bullet points to provide detail

- models or charts to convey complex concepts

- appendices (not all relevant information needs to be included in the body of the document)

- project or implementation plans that capture the detail.

Get your team on board

In this book we explore a broad range of strategies and approaches to inspire your team to become fully engaged with your organisation and their own role. What we will focus on here is what it takes to ensure your team understand and are committed to achieving your vision and strategy. The most important outcome you need to achieve is to instil across your team a sense of personal ownership of the plan and the results ultimately created.

Priority 1: involve your team

Too many organisations rely purely on their leaders to develop strategic plans. Involving other team members, however, allows you to leverage their insights and contributes to building a sense of ownership of your plans at every level of your team. Most people understand you can't and won't adopt every idea they have; what matters is that they feel they have been allowed to contribute. They need to know that their views and ideas are valued and have been given serious consideration.

There are lots of different ways you can get your team involved, including through surveys, focus groups and working committees. It can also be as simple as asking people to volunteer their ideas during team meetings. Your approach doesn't need to be complex, time consuming or labour intensive; you just need to ask for, capture and consider your team's point of view.

Priority 2: assign accountability

Reflect for a moment on when you have attended a planning workshop, spending a day or more discussing important issues and making resolutions, only to come back to work and fail to implement what you had agreed to. This is a common challenge and reflects why so often vision and strategy-planning exercises fail. Agreeing who is responsible for key outcomes and specific initiatives is the first step towards holding people accountable for making them happen. Unless you have these commitments in place it is all too easy to become distracted by the day to day and fail to deliver on your longer term plans.

Once you have finalised your plan it's important to agree on the next-step priorities and on when you will reconvene to check on progress. People need to understand there will be a review of their progress and they will be held to account for things they are asked to deliver on. Of course it is important to be reasonable and flexible but, as we will explore in greater depth in chapter 6, applying consequences is an important external motivator of compliance.

Priority 3: communicate

In chapter 5 we will look more closely at how communication influences your ability to earn the buy-in of people on your team and other important stakeholders. For now it is important to reflect on the role of communication in ensuring that your team understand and support your vision and strategy. By actively involving your team in the process you will be off to a good start, but maintaining awareness, understanding and acceptance are important priorities of your communication strategy. Focus your communications efforts on making sure every member of your team understands:

- what your vision for the future is
- key strategic objectives and priorities
- the major initiatives and projects that will be undertaken
- the role every member of the team is expected to play
- how you will respond to change, challenge and obstacles.

Communicating your vision and strategy is far from a one-off or annual event; your team should be constantly kept abreast of progress and priorities. Information can come from the CEO or a senior executive, but for people to fully engage, typically it is important for people to also hear it from their direct manager. A critical priority for you as a people manager is the ways in which you keep your team informed and help them to understand the links between your organisation's plans and what each member personally needs to contribute.

Chapter summary: the most important things to do and avoid

Must-do checklist

The most important things you must do to establish and leverage an effective vision and strategy include the following:

✓ dare to dream big and challenge conventional wisdom

✓ adopt a dynamic and ongoing approach to your planning efforts

✓ involve your team and keep them informed

(continued)

Chapter summary (cont'd)

✓ work out the plan to get to your destination and implement it with discipline

✓ understand and plan for the obstacles and risks that may lie ahead

✓ be flexible and responsive to changing circumstances

✓ monitor and measure your progress.

Common mistakes to avoid

The most common mistakes I observe people managers make that undermine their ability to establish and leverage an effective vision and strategy include:

✗ limiting potential through fear and unfounded belief

✗ treating vision and strategy as a planning event rather than as tools needing constant review and refinement

✗ allowing flexibility and agility to lead to a lack of focus or uncertainty

✗ becoming bogged down in detailed plans and documents

✗ paralysis due to over-analysis

✗ perfectionism: allowing the absence of the perfect plan to hold you back from moving forward.

Chapter 3

Culture

A primary task in taking a company from good to great is to create a culture wherein people have a tremendous opportunity to be heard and ultimately, for the truth to be heard.

Jim Collins, best-selling author of *Good to Great* (2001)

The environment created in any workplace has a significant impact on the spirit and performance of the people who work there. Not only does the environment we work in influence the strength of our passion and energy, but it plays a major role in determining how we choose to behave. Far more than simply affecting the way we feel, the cultural environment of any workplace has the power to set the standard of everyone's conduct and performance. A strong culture—good or bad—will influence each person, reinforcing and entrenching patterns of behaviour. For this reason, it can be extremely challenging to shift a culture once it has been created.

In this chapter we will explore:

- designing the culture you want to create
- identifying the values and behaviours that will enable you to achieve your objectives

- the importance of setting clear behavioural expectations and leading by example

- why applying consequences consistently through remedial action and reward is critical.

Think for a moment how often you have worked in an atmosphere that inspires you to be better than you are or to achieve more ambitious goals. When, if ever, have you experienced a culture that motivated you to be loyal despite constant challenges and battles in your job? When have you worked in or witnessed a team with a culture that sapped enthusiasm or lowered the bar on what was possible for everyone in the group? I have personally experienced each of these scenarios. I also regularly observe them in operation through the teams and organisations I work with.

Culture is created from the collective behaviours of people in a given setting or group. It can be described as the way things are typically done or as the personality of the organisation. The culture of a business is not about the way things should be in theory but about the way they are in practice. The decisions made, the priorities set, the actions taken — all provide insight into the culture of a team or business. An important driver of any culture created is the desire most people have to succeed. When we join a team most of us consciously and unconsciously look for signals that tell us what the most valued and successful behaviours are in that environment. While, of course, some people don't care to do things in ways that will allow them to fit in and be accepted, most people look to align with the approaches adopted by their colleagues, approaches they perceive will enable them to be accepted, valued and ultimately successful.

Our desire to assimilate with our environment influences our behavioural choices, as does the impact we feel from the collective spirit of the team we are a part of. When teams are energised, and have a deep reserve of positive energy, individuals typically choose behaviours that are more positive and enabling of success. In contrast, groups drained of spirit are more likely to elect to behave in ways that undermine their ability to achieve their own objectives. In turn, these poor behavioural choices are likely to impact upon the spirit of other people and influence the choices they in turn make about how to behave. Just as a strong and energised spirit is likely to positively influence the ways in which people and teams behave, a drained spirit inspires negative behaviours in most people.

What success looks like

The ultimate indicator of the effectiveness of your culture management efforts is the performance of your business. Here are some direct measures of the success of your workplace culture:

- People consistently behave in ways that are aligned with the values of your business.
- Trust, respect, integrity and accountability are reflected in your cultural values.
- Your staff stay because they love working for your business and don't want to go anywhere else.
- You have a strong reputation in the market for being the kind of place where people want to work.
- Prospective employees proactively seek out opportunities to work with you.

Here are some of the key indicators of a well-executed culture management strategy and practice:

- In all hiring decisions priority is given to culture fit.
- Leaders walk the talk and are a positive example of your culture.
- People are assessed not only on what they achieve but on how they go about it.

(continued)

What success looks like (cont'd)

- Cultural misalignment is taken seriously and addressed.

- Every member of the team, irrespective of seniority, performance or any privileged position, is expected to behave in line with your business values.

Case study
Follow the leader

For many years I have worked with Bill, the CEO of a manufacturing business that has enjoyed rapid growth and expansion year on year. When we first began working together Bill had a relatively small team of 65 people working at one site. Today Bill's team has grown to approximately 280 people located at three sites. What began as a singularly focused business has grown to one capable of offering a wide range of products to a relatively diverse client base.

A number of years ago Bill asked me to undertake a review and provide him with feedback about how things were going through the eyes of his team. Bill wanted to know what the team perceived as their strengths and how they believed things needed to improve. In particular, Bill wanted to understand the impacts of growth on his team and their performance. While he didn't have any specific concerns Bill was anxious to check in with his staff and understand current reality as perceived by them.

While on the surface things appeared to be going very well, discussions with Bill's team soon revealed cracks beginning to appear. It was clear some members of the team were struggling to keep pace in what had quickly become a much larger and more complex business. Systems and processes struggled to cope with greater volume, staff lacked the skills and experience needed to consistently deliver, and people's work overload led to a lack of the communication and collaboration critical to pulling the team together.

It was equally clear that some managers were feeling the stress of not only leading their team but also meeting the demands of their growing client base. Daniel, the Sales Manager, stood out as one leader who was struggling with the demands of his job. Appointed to the management role based largely on his sales performance and knowledge of the market, Daniel was well equipped to guide the team's sales strategy and approach to winning new business.

What Daniel wasn't prepared or equipped for was the task of engaging with and managing the people on his team. He appeared even less prepared for the need to lead the way and build close working relationships with other people across the business. Daniel struggled to engage effectively with not only members of his own team but also those working in client service, production and finance roles. The consequences were serious and wide ranging; Daniel's problems were clearly having a significant impact on morale and on the culture of the business.

Daniel is a textbook example of someone who while meeting his performance targets was falling well short of the behavioural standards expected of him. Especially disappointing was the clearly observable breakdown in relationships among members of the sales team and between them and other departments. What's more, some people showed clear signs of adopting Daniel's style and approach.

The general tone of communications had become aggressive and defensive, client service team members were quick to avoid accountability and looked for reasons to blame sales people for breakdowns in the process, and production staff flatly refused to visit the sales area when previously their interactions had been regular and routine. As Bill's organisation grew, so too did a culture of blame; as their world became busier and more complex, their culture of respect and collaboration was being eroded. While Daniel wasn't solely responsible for these cultural challenges, in his senior leadership position he had significant influence.

Bill struggled at first with how to broach the issue with Daniel; his main fear was upsetting Daniel and potentially even losing him to the competition. Bill argued that Daniel was under a lot of pressure and saw this as the driving force behind his aggressive, disrespectful and often sarcastic approach to dealing with people. For some months Bill left Daniel's poor conduct unaddressed and simply hoped that over time he would learn better coping mechanisms.

Things did change, but unfortunately for the worse. Progressively Daniel's conduct deteriorated to a point where Bill could no longer bury his head in the sand and hope it would go away. Bill found the courage to have a frank and yet compassionate discussion with Daniel about how he was behaving and the impact this was having on the spirit of the team and culture of the business. Bill shared with me later that Daniel quickly became emotional and opened up about the stress and anxiety he had been feeling since taking on the sales leadership role.

Daniel was honest about his dislike of leading people and the frustrations he felt in having to deal with their issues. Bill was surprised by Daniel's frank confession. Daniel shared that while he was aware his conduct was out of order, he struggled to be different. While he didn't articulate it in these terms, his behaviour was clear evidence that Daniel's spirit was drained.

The success story here is the decisions that were made from this point on. Daniel and Bill recognised they had two options: either Daniel improved his conduct dramatically or he could no longer work as the sales manager. Daniel requested that Bill consider allowing him to return to the individual contributor position he had formally held. Acknowledging that regardless of the role he assumed he needed to behave in line with the organisation's values, Daniel was eager to move back to a role he enjoyed and in which he had been successful.

Eager to keep Daniel in the business, Bill agreed and the change was made with immediate effect. Some months after these events Bill shared with me the enormity of the lesson he had learned from this experience. Bill told me, 'Daniel isn't meant to be a people leader. He doesn't enjoy it and isn't good at it'. Bill had realised that the core of Daniel's success was his happiness in his role and that putting the wrong person in a people management role can have a profound impact on the culture and spirit of the entire team. Bill vowed that he would never again appoint someone to a leadership role who wasn't well suited to, as well as qualified for, the job.

Adopting a strategic approach

The real value of a strategic approach to managing culture is reflected in your ability to attract and retain great people and create competitive advantage. Both winning the so-called 'war for talent' and differentiating yourself in what are more often than not competitive landscapes are powerful reasons for placing priority on the culture of your team or business. Even if your organisation doesn't need to compete for business, you are likely to need to compete for talent. A not-for-profit organisation, for example, may not be driven to maximise financial results, but it needs talented and energised people on the team as much as the most commercially focused enterprise.

The culture of a business can prove to be a significant competitive advantage. Given enough time, money and resources your competitors can easily duplicate or take almost everything you do or are good at. They can copy your products or services, reverse engineer your processes and even steal your sales and marketing ideas. However, replicating the behaviours, relationships, attitudes and values your people bring is a challenge that may be possible in theory but is highly unlikely in practice. The uniqueness and strength of your culture create the opportunity for you to differentiate your business and set you apart from others in your industry.

Attracting and retaining talented people in a competitive market with potentially greener pastures all around them is an important priority for any business. This war for talent is fought both within and outside of your organisation. The cultural environment you provide will be a major influence on whether members of your team choose to stay even if approached with an attractive offer to work somewhere else. Equally, the cultural environment a prospective employer can offer weighs heavily on the decisions people make about whether they will join a new team.

One strategy to winning the war for talent adopted by many organisations is to become an employer of choice. Much has been written about what that means and how to go about achieving it. Despite the complexity of many of the models and frameworks that are said to underlie it, being an employer of choice is in fact a far from complicated concept. It simply means people want to work for you, love it when they get there and want to stay. The cultural environment you offer underpins how people feel about working for you.

Organisations that understand the powerful impact culture has on their success adopt a planned and deliberate approach to influencing the attitudes and behaviours prevalent in their business. Not only do they proactively establish and clearly articulate what they stand for and how they expect people to behave, but they ensure leaders are skilled and able to positively influence their culture. As we will explore in the sections ahead, designing your culture and proactively driving its creation are critical priorities for all people managers. Every manager plays an important role in turning the organisation's cultural aspirations into reality.

Design your culture

Leveraging maximum value from the culture in your workplace comes down to your ability to influence the behaviours you need people to bring to their roles — in other words, inspiring the types of conduct and approaches that will enable your whole team to succeed. Next we will explore the most important things you can do to create the type of culture that supports your objectives. While it is important that your culture be tailored to your unique needs and circumstances, we will also explore the characteristics of a healthy workplace culture that underpin the success of any group of people in any setting. There is no such thing as the ideal culture, but some values enable an environment where people are most likely to feel valued and respected, and therefore to thrive.

Priority 1: understand the culture you want to create

The first step to deliberately influencing culture is to understand what you are trying to create. As with anything you want to achieve, establishing a clear vision of where you want to go will help you determine the best path to take you there. It isn't enough simply to say, for example, that you want a high-performance culture. You need to clearly articulate what 'high-performance' means in your business. Does it relate to quality, growth or service, or all of those things? In the sections ahead we will explore how to identify the values and behaviours unique to your own organisation's needs. Before we do, however, let's first consider the attributes of a healthy culture that all organisations should aspire to.

Perfect culture

While it is true to say there is no perfect culture to which organisations should aspire, working with businesses of all sizes, at varying stages of their development and across a broad range of industries, has shown me the importance of some fundamental values that underpin the type of culture most likely to inspire the best from people. The core values of trust, respect and accountability form an important foundation upon which positive and high-performing workplace cultures are created. Each in turn influences the extent to which people and teams embrace other important values such as integrity, teamwork and commitment to quality.

Trust and respect for our boss and colleagues, for example, will typically influence the extent to which we are willing to be honest about our thoughts and feelings or even present an authentic version of ourselves at work. Our willingness to collaborate or support others to succeed is underpinned by feeling trust and respect towards and from the people we work with. Equally, both trust and respect affect how likely we are to be loyal and inspired to strive through challenging times.

Accountability focuses people on achieving results and encourages them to strive to overcome barriers to success. Tapping into personal ownership and discretionary effort is a characteristic of an environment where people feel responsible for the contributions they make. It is important that people feel good about working in your business, but ultimately they are there to get a job done. An absence of accountability in a respectful environment can lead to a congenial culture that nonetheless yields sub-optimal performance.

Organisations must focus on the unique values and behaviours most likely to contribute to their ability to succeed, but the list should always include those that are likely to encourage ethical behaviours, nurture the human spirit and drive performance.

Priority 2: identify core values

The conventions of professional conduct in business require that you set expectations and hold people accountable for behaving in ways that may reasonably be understood as reflecting a spirit of cooperation and good intention. The purpose of core values is to communicate the attitudes, beliefs and behaviours considered most important to the success of your business. They provide a powerful reference point for what is desirable, beneficial, important and ultimately accepted.

To make them effective, limit the values you focus on to those considered most essential. Values lose impact when there are too many and people struggle to recall even what they are, let alone what they mean. As a rule of thumb, you are likely to find that somewhere between four and seven core values is the right number for your business. There is an endless array of options to choose from; what matters is that you select those values that best articulate the approaches to working that will enable you to achieve your objectives.

Reflect on your organisation's vision and strategy, and consider the types of attitudes and behaviours that will enable you to succeed. For example, is being innovative and coming up with new and improved ways of doing things important to achieving your goals, or is it more important that your team are keenly focused on maturing your approaches and protecting you against risk? Perhaps both matter. Or does your business achieve competitive advantage through ensuring that your clients experience a responsive and flexible approach when dealing with members of your team? If so a culture based on service excellence may be your most important priority. Reflect on the values that are at the heart of the types of behaviours you want to encourage and hold people accountable for.

As a people manager working in a business with defined values, your role becomes to ensure every member of your team understands what these values mean in practice. In other words, you may not be in a position to decide what values matter most, but you are able to leverage them to optimal effect through the example you set, the expectations you hold and the actions you take. As we will explore in the following sections, the discipline with which these values are reinforced plays a critical role in creating the culture you want.

Priority 3: define behaviours

Every member of your team needs to understand how to behave in ways considered not only acceptable but also conducive to success in your organisation. Identifying your core values is only the first step; next you need to model behaviours to illustrate them. For example, if integrity is an important core value in your business you must describe what it looks like in action. One organisation I work with focuses on the following behaviours to define what it means to them to act with integrity:

- Be honest and respectful when dealing with others.

- Do what we say and hold ourselves accountable.

- Be fair in all of our dealings and interactions.

- Demonstrate empathy and be considerate.

In another business I have worked with the behaviours used to describe integrity are very different but just as relevant:

- Focus on our clients and keep promises we make.

- Be honest, open and transparent.

- Think of others and consider the impact of our actions.

- Lead by example.

More often than not it is possible to come up with a long list of behaviours that reflect a particular value. What matters is selecting four or five key behaviours that set the tone for what is expected and accepted.

Priority 4: get your team involved

Engaging your team in the process of identifying your values and behaviours is an important opportunity to influence the level of their engagement and buy-in. The role every member of your team plays in designing your culture influences how they choose to behave and, ultimately, the impact they have on your success. It's not just leaders who need to be involved; every person in your group, irrespective of their position, needs to contribute and to comply with your values for them to have any real meaning. Even the least experienced member of your team can provide valuable insight into what matters and will work, and even the longest serving staffer must adopt your values for you to have any chance of creating the culture you want.

There are many different approaches you can take, some of which will be affected by the size of your team and practicalities of getting people involved. The primary objective you should focus on is ensuring that everyone feels they have had a voice in the process. It doesn't matter whether or not everyone agrees; what matters is that everyone believes they were given the opportunity to share their thoughts about the process. People are much more likely to feel a sense of emotional ownership of the outcomes, regardless of what they may be, if their voice has been heard and seriously considered. Examples of the ways in which you can involve team members include:

- questionnaires
- focus groups or workshops
- working committees made up of staff representatives from across your business
- tapping into feedback through team meetings
- inviting staff to volunteer suggestions, for example via email.

One organisation I work with identified broadly the attributes of the culture they wanted to create and then leveraged their entire team to come up with values and behaviours to support it. To be clear, this was a relatively small organisation that was able to convene team meetings to gain direct input from every person. Another chose first to establish their cultural vision and values among the senior leadership team. From there, each executive worked with managers and staff in their division to decide what each value meant to them in practice. Each team focused on and were held accountable for their own set of behaviours. For example, to the marketing team innovation had a very different meaning from the one held by accounting. In fact, the teams with a strong compliance focus had a vastly different view of what it means to be innovative from those in highly creative roles.

These differences are valid and worth understanding; after all, there is no point asking people to focus their behaviours in ways that are irrelevant, valueless and even counterproductive to the fundamental objectives they know they need to achieve. Regardless of how you choose to engage your team, what matters is that you do. Nothing will have as great an impact on your team as feeling collective ownership of the culture they have played a part in creating.

As time moves on new members of your team will not have been involved; what matters then is that their colleagues are willing and able to say, 'These are the behaviours we all signed up for because they are important to us'. When other team members proactively lead by example and consistently behave in line with your values because they believe in them, then you are likely to have achieved the traction needed to embed your values in the way things are done in your business.

Priority 5: watch your language

The words used to define your culture should resonate with and make sense to the people working in your business. Values and behaviours should be articulated in ways that people understand as more than a bunch of words from the dictionary of management jargon. If not used effectively, language can be both confusing and off-putting, unnecessarily creating obstacles to winning buy-in from your team. For example, the language used by a professional services team can contrast starkly with that used by people working in an industrial environment.

Here are a couple of examples from organisations I have worked with. Quality for one team was expressed as meaning to 'Proactively challenge ourselves to be focused on the accuracy of everything we do' and in another, 'Do it right the first time'. Knowing both of these teams, I can affirm they shared a desire to communicate the importance of avoiding errors, but they chose to express that desire in very different words—the language they felt their respective teams were best able to relate to. Similarly, in defining innovation, one team said, 'Push the boundaries and question everything we do to enable us to continually improve', while another said, 'Think outside the square'.

It is virtually impossible to document everything a value can mean in practice; neither is it practical to attempt to capture every behaviour that illustrates a value you are working to reinforce. What is important is that the team get it and know what they need to do. Of course, written statements can go some way to achieving clarity, but getting people involved is far more valuable. Just as important are the conversations people managers have with their team to help them understand and consistently demonstrate the behaviours expected.

Drive your culture

New organisations may look to establish a strong culture and maintain it as they grow. Rapidly-growing organisations may need to safeguard against cultural challenges that commonly arise when ambitious people are striving to move forward quickly. For other organisations their goals may be to shift an entrenched culture to enable them to improve performance or change direction. Of course, each of these scenarios could relate to a team within a business. Regardless of the primary objective or drivers behind your culture management efforts, establishing a clear plan that is understood and owned by every people manager responsible for driving culture is fundamental to success.

Priority 1: understand and face your current reality

Once you intimately understand the culture you want, next you need to recognise the gaps between where you are now and where you want to be. In other words, how different or far from your vision is your current reality? With this understanding you are in a position to identify the priorities and approaches needed to successfully drive your culture in the right direction. Over the years, I have worked with a lot of managers who are on the one hand eager to improve their team culture but on the other hesitant to face reality honestly. Often motivated by fear of exposing problems they will then have to deal with, these managers avoid the issue altogether.

Although this is certainly not always the case, some managers are simply reluctant to hear the things people may say about their management style or approach. As difficult as it may feel in the moment, managers need to face the truth about the impact they personally have on the culture of their team or business. It is not at all uncommon for business owners or CEOs to ask me to help them shift a culture that is clearly and profoundly influenced by their own values and behaviours. More often than not in these circumstances coaching the senior leader to adapt their own way of working is fundamental to enabling them to achieve their culture change objectives.

As we will explore in greater depth in 'Priority 3: drive from the top', the way the most senior person chooses to behave, the decisions they make and actions they take, is the primary driver of culture in any organisation.

Priority 2: set clear expectations

Once you establish a clear view of the ways in which you want people to behave, you need to tell them. This may seem too obvious a point to warrant a mention, but it's extraordinary how often I encounter managers who fail to communicate the behaviours they and their organisation expect. Even when they understand those behaviours and have them clearly written down, some managers fail to discuss them with their team. Many managers fail to invest the energy needed even to communicate the outcomes and targets their people are aiming for, let alone how they are expected to conduct themselves.

Setting clear, well-understood expectations is the first step towards being in a position to hold people accountable for appropriate behaviours and standards of conduct. There should be no doubt in anyone's mind about what these are. While there is some value in company- or team-wide communications, leaders must engage with each individual member of their team to confirm that they understand what is expected of them. Providing this clarity needs to begin with leaders; each needs to understand intimately the role they personally must play to drive the culture.

Priority 3: drive from the top

While creating or shifting the culture can be challenging and people can be complex, the formula for success is not. Success is intimately related to the degree of real and visible ownership embraced from the top. More than just owning the culture, managers need to represent the best example of the culture they are working to create. It is a non-negotiable requirement for every leader, from the CEO through to each and every people manager, to lead by example and to be a champion of the desired workplace culture. John Kotter, an expert on leadership and transformation, sums it up perfectly: 'If the requirements for promotion don't change, renewal rarely lasts. One bad succession decision at the top of an organisation can undermine a decade of hard work'.

No-one should ever be appointed to a leadership role unless they operate in ways consistent with the culture you want to create or maintain. Leadership capability and accountability are both crucial and together have the greatest impact on success. Developing an organisation's culture requires that leaders showcase the behaviours that are expected from everyone, whether that means putting in effort, demonstrating a positive attitude, dealing with conflicts constructively or helping a colleague to get their job done. For behaviours to become entrenched, people need to see their leaders consistently display those behaviours. For example, team members are far more likely to go above and beyond the tasks defined by their job descriptions if they observe leaders doing the same. It's important to remember that when you lead by example, you create a picture not only of what's desirable but also of what's possible.

CEO — custodian of culture

Like any member of a team, the most senior person has an important and specific role to play to enable the success of the group. For ease of reference I will refer to the person in this role as the CEO, but what we will explore here relates equally to the head of a team, department or division. As the expression 'the fish always rots from the head down' graphically implies, a team will never have an effective culture unless the approach from the top is what it needs to be. As a leader of leaders, a senior manager has even greater influence and responsibility.

Before we look more closely at the role a CEO plays, it's important to acknowledge the influence a board of directors can have in some businesses. Depending on circumstances, the board can play a major role in defining the culture of the business through the priorities, decisions and actions they take. The expectations they have of the CEO and their determination to hold him accountable for creating a successful workplace culture are critical. It can be difficult for a CEO to get the job done when faced with a board that places little value on culture or the spirit of the team.

This can be particularly true in some public companies that focus on financial results with little appreciation of the impact of culture on performance and sustainability. Peter, one CEO I worked with, struggled to win board approval to invest in resources that would enable him to dramatically improve their culture and subsequent performance. Newly appointed to his role, Peter recognised the importance of leadership development and HR support to achieve the culture change objectives needed to overcome performance challenges they had been facing—the very challenges Peter had been hired to overcome. Members of the board, however, were hesitant to invest in these priorities. While challenging, it is incumbent upon the CEO in these circumstances to work hard to influence the board's understanding of culture and its influence on business results.

Leadership capability

While a lot of managers proactively and conscientiously drive the culture of their team, many don't. Beyond simply an issue of commitment or interest, many of the managers I work with lack the knowledge, skills and experience needed. While they understand their role and want to do a good job, they lack the necessary know-how and confidence. This is one of the most significant obstacles to success I have observed. If you are a manager of managers, provide them with the training, coaching, advice or guidance they need. Help the people managers who work for you to play their role effectively by equipping them with the depth of capability needed. Consider also the support that can be provided by HR people on your team, by external advisers or consultants or by more experienced members of your leadership team. If you are a people manager struggling to work out how to develop your team's culture, seek out the advice and support you need. Prioritise learning solutions that will guide your development and commit fully to leveraging their full benefit.

Priority 4: make it matter

The next important priority is taking the theory of driving culture and putting it into practice. For values and behaviours to have any real impact on the culture of your team you can't just say they matter; they need to *really* matter. There must be consequences. Consequences are about rewarding and recognising successful behaviours as much as about taking remedial action when needed. It can be easy to advocate the values and behaviours people should bring to their work, but any real impact you have on culture is driven by the extent to which your actions are aligned with your words.

A key reason I observe for failed culture change initiatives is talking without doing. Too much time is spent talking about the culture we want, values that are important, behaviours expected, role of the managers, right steps to take and so on. But often too little is invested in having the conversations, making the decisions and acting deliberately to ensure people behave in ways that enable success. Little or nothing is gained from articulating core values and expected behaviours unless you are willing to hold people accountable for them. The way you set priorities, make decisions and implement actions communicates volumes to your team about how much behaving in line with your culture really matters.

Another common mistake organisations make is to place too strong a focus on HR-driven culture change programs. Any culture program that isn't owned by people managers is destined to fail and can even adversely impact on the spirit of the team. Espousing values or behaviours that are not clearly and consistently supported by managers can annoy and even anger people. Perceived as broken promises, unfulfilled values are a constant reminder that the organisation promised to be better than it is today. Over time people and teams lose all hope and come to see the values as a disappointing reflection of what the organisation could be or an infuriating reflection of the organisation's hypocrisy.

To be clear, it is entirely appropriate to articulate aspirational values and behaviours, but buy-in is undermined when people observe little genuine effort is made to ensure they are applied, especially by managers. It's important to acknowledge gaps between the team culture you want to create and the way people already behave. Failing then to do anything about driving change will grossly undermine the confidence people have in the sincerity of your intentions and commitment. People are observant, and when they see accountability applied they are more likely to believe in where the organisation's culture is heading.

At times even HR-owned and -driven culture programs add value; typically, however, this is limited to developing awareness of the culture needed to drive success. Some culture programs outline how to create the culture by providing a framework upon which each manager can base their approach. Although many of these programs are well structured, written and documented, few are implemented effectively and fewer still achieve their objectives. The value of the program is ultimately limited to the extent to which every people manager applies it to the way they lead their team.

Value both what people do and how they do it

Valuing not only the things people are able to achieve but also how they go about it is the single most important thing a manager can do to drive the culture of their team. No matter what incredible results people achieve, the way they behave must be an equally important part of your assessment of their performance. Often leaders will say to me, 'I'm having trouble with a team member's behaviour but can't fault her performance. How do I handle this?' This question reflects what I commonly observe as a tendency for some managers to define performance within the limited scope of outcomes achieved. Unless both outcomes and behaviours are central to the expectations we set and the appraisals we make of people, we are unlikely to build the culture we want or achieve outstanding results.

Apply consequences

How often have you observed managers claim their organisation stands for something and then fail to lead by example or to hold people accountable for aligned behaviours? All too often I witness managers and whole management teams who struggle to model or enforce the values and behaviours they say they expect. Setting a good example and enforcing accountability must happen if values are to become absorbed into the way things are done in a business. The discipline with which these values are reinforced through applied consequences plays a critical role in creating your organisation or team culture.

Consequences are not just remedial, such as reprimanding or punishing people for behaving in ways you don't want them to. Creating an organisation's culture means reinforcing the behaviours you want to see as much as deterring those you don't. Catching people doing things well, and deliberately rewarding and recognising their contributions, has an important impact on encouraging others to follow suit.

Be consistent

Culture cannot be deliberately influenced without a consistent approach. Consistency both across the management team and from one member of your team to another is critical to success. Inconsistency undermines any manager's credibility and therefore their ability to influence their team's culture. That said, however, maintaining a consistent approach can be difficult to achieve in practice. Consistency demands a common understanding and application across all people managers. It also demands that managers have the courage to address behaviour issues irrespective of the team member in question.

Among the more courageous and productive things I see managers do is to call out the poor behaviours of high-achieving staff. Addressing the inappropriate behaviours of team members who excel at achieving targets or have rare skill sets can be challenging for a lot of managers. Many are hesitant to step into what they perceive to be treacherous territory. However, finding the courage to do so can be one of the most important things a manager does to influence the culture. Some of these individuals perceive themselves to be 'untouchable' and therefore feel no obligation to comply with behavioural expectations. Holding them accountable is one of the strongest signals a leader can send to both them and others about non-negotiable values and behaviours.

Recruit for fit

Every member of your team brings their personal values and beliefs to work everyday. The ways in which they choose to behave are the observable and measurable manifestations of these values and beliefs. As we will explore in greater depth in chapter 4, the decisions you make about the values you hire into your business matter as much to your success in building a great workplace culture as the steps you take to reward, recognise or redress behaviours.

Assessing each candidate's alignment with your core values must be given priority in any recruitment process. However attractive the knowledge, skills and experience of a candidate may be, if you are not confident they will bring aligned values and behaviours, don't hire them. Hiring people with values that are not aligned with those you wish to promote can have devastating consequences for your culture that may take years to uproot. To ensure you have indeed made the right hiring decisions, consider your recruitment process complete only after the candidate has successfully worked through a probationary period of employment (if applicable in the region in which you work).

Identify and address cultural misalignment

From time to time, despite your best efforts, you are likely to have people on your team who struggle to fit in with your culture. Even when you focus on culture through your hiring process, establish clear expectations upfront when people join and provide constructive feedback along the way, some people will behave in ways that undermine or threaten the health of your culture. Even one member of a team behaving badly can have a significant impact on your culture and team, and once identified the problem should be immediately addressed.

Sometimes taking action simply means providing feedback or coaching that helps someone to understand how they need to shift their approach. At other times your intervention may need to be more involved or serious. Ultimately, if after giving the person a fair and reasonable opportunity to change they still don't fit your culture, you need to exit them from your business.

We are not talking here about perfection but rather that they are able to behave in line with your core values. Even the most aligned team member is likely to lapse occasionally into unacceptable conduct. Exiting someone becomes necessary when they clearly do not share the values of your business and are therefore unlikely to succeed in your environment.

Chapter summary: the most important things to do and avoid

Must-do checklist

The most important things you must do to create a culture that enables success are:

✓ take ownership and lead by example; be a visible champion through mindset and behaviour

✓ clearly define cultural aspirations

✓ understand and confront cultural reality: explore the full truth about how things really are

✓ identify the values and behaviours that underpin the culture you want

✓ expect every team member to conduct themselves in line with your values and behaviours

✓ mandate, endorse and enforce agreed strategies, programs and policies

✓ send clear and consistent messages, through words and actions, about what really matters

✓ monitor, measure and assess behaviour for alignment

✓ apply consequences: reward and recognise, or take remedial action.

Common mistakes to avoid

The most common mistakes I observe people managers make that undermine their ability to influence the culture of their team successfully include:

✗ espousing values that they fail to demonstrate; people would rather you didn't make a promise than fail to follow through

✗ expecting culture to be driven by HR people; every leader must be on board and actively driving the culture

✗ using posters or written statements to communicate cultural expectations without one-on-one or team-based discussions to ensure understanding

✗ failing to take action: managing culture takes a dynamic and hands-on approach. Just because you have written down and communicated expectations doesn't mean your job is done.

Chapter 4

Recruitment

I am convinced that nothing we do is more important than hiring and developing people. At the end of the day you bet on people, not on strategies.

Lawrence Bossidy, former chairman and CEO of AlliedSignal Corporation

The decisions you make about who to appoint to each role are crucial not only to the individual's success but also to the performance of your business as a whole. Whether recruiting from within or outside your organisation, appointing talented people who bring culturally aligned values and behaviours underpins your ability to achieve great results through your team. Far more than merely an operational process focused on filling vacant roles, recruitment has significant immediate and longer term impacts on any business and must be seen as a strategic priority.

In this chapter we will explore:

- developing talent pools that enable you to find the right people when you need them
- how to identify the most important capabilities and attributes needed in a role

- the hallmarks of a successful recruitment process

- assessing the competence and cultural alignment of potential employees

- what it takes to get the best from the recruitment consultants you work with.

While far from the only contributing factor, many of the people challenges managers face can be traced back to poor recruitment decisions. Appointing people who are unqualified, unprepared or reluctant to take on the demands of a role inevitably leads to substandard performance and often costly mistakes. Hiring people who drain the spirit of your team and induce a culture of inappropriate behaviour can lead you down a path that is fatal to the success, if not the viability, of your business.

When you get recruitment right the positive effects are profound. Appointing people who are capable, energised, optimistic, driven and respectful not only brings strength to their role but also influences the success of others around them. The right people can bring both knowledge and behaviours that help a team turn their performance around. In this chapter we will focus on the most important things you can do to ensure you make the right hiring decisions every time. We will also explore the common pitfalls and obstacles to success and how to avoid them.

What success looks like

The ultimate indicator of the effectiveness of your recruitment strategy and practices is the performance of your business. Measures of both the quality of your hiring decisions and the effectiveness of your process are included in the following lists.

(continued)

What success looks like (cont'd)

Key indicators of high-quality hiring decisions include
the following:

- Behaviours of new team members are strongly aligned
  with the values of the business.

- Promoted staff contribute to a positive and productive
  workplace culture.

- Successful candidates are able to perform the role to the
  standard expected.

- Newly appointed staff quickly and fully integrate into
  their team and the organisation.

- New team members have the ability to grow with their
  role and the organisation.

- Most new staff commit to the role for at least two years.

Key indicators of high-quality recruitment include
the following:

- A well-planned and consistent approach is adopted
  throughout.

- No adverse impacts to operations are experienced because
  of capability or resource gaps.

- Time and cost objectives are met.

- Recruits understand the key objectives and responsibilities
  of their role.

- Candidates express satisfaction that they have been
  provided with a fair and lawful opportunity.

- All candidates have a positive perception of your business
  and culture.

Case study
Fit for purpose

Among the most important recruitment decisions an organisation makes are those relating to the leaders they promote or invite to join their team. How often have you observed a newly appointed leader influence the success and even the wellbeing of a team? While the suitability of every person hired matters, leaders in particular can have a direct impact on the success of others through the priorities they set, the decisions they make and the actions they take. They set an example of what is expected and what is accepted, and ultimately dictate the extent to which a cohesive and high-performing team is even considered important, let alone realised.

While consulting to a financial services organisation I witnessed a powerful example of the importance of getting recruitment right. A publicly listed company with close to 350 staff nationally had been struggling for a number of years to improve the engagement and performance of their team. Their engagement results had been declining for years, and they faced growing challenges in both attracting and retaining talented people. The engagement survey they conducted shortly before we met revealed that only 23 per cent of staff at that time were willing to recommend the organisation as a good place to work. The most common reason people gave for leaving was the organisation's culture — in particular, the way they had been managed.

While the organisation's challenges were clearly not the fault of the CEO, Michael, alone, he had played a lead role in creating them both through his own behaviour and in failing to manage others effectively. When Michael abruptly and unexpectedly left the business a search to find his replacement began. Recognising the opportunity they had to substantially improve performance, the board placed an uncompromisingly strong focus on people leadership capabilities.

The search and assessment process adopted was robust, to say the least. Candidates who did not demonstrate a solid track record of leading successful teams were simply not considered. Those who did make the cut were asked to participate in a series of interviews not only with members of the board but also with selected general managers who were regarded both as high performers and as aligned with the organisation's desired culture. Psychometric testing and extensive reference checking were also important tools leveraged in the assessment and selection process adopted.

Six months after Michael's departure it was announced that a new CEO, Stephen, had been appointed. By this time morale was at an all-time low and turnover at an all-time high. It is reasonable to conclude that most people waited with a degree of trepidation for the new CEO to start. Talk among the troops was heavily focused on what Stephen would bring to the role and whether the organisation would change or continue to operate as it had.

In stark contrast to Michael, Stephen brought with him a philosophy that every member of the team was critical to success. While he advocated a compassionate and respectful approach to leading people, he placed equal focus on accountability. Stephen believed that the number one priority of every leader was to influence the success of each individual on their team. Just as important was his view that while leadership mattered, every team member must also take personal ownership of not only their own success but the success of their teammates too.

Over time the approach Stephen adopted had a significant impact on the spirit of the team, and while some people were asked to leave those who remained reported a growing sense of loyalty and commitment. In the time I worked closely with that organisation I observed staff turnover plummet from a high of 36 per cent to 16 per cent. Significant progress on many of the organisation's strategic priorities was also clearly apparent. While further work needed to be done to achieve the success they were striving for, it was easy to see the profoundly positive impact Stephen's appointment to the role of CEO had had on that business.

Stephen's appointment is just one example of getting the recruitment process right. Unfortunately, all too often I have also observed the consequences of poor hiring decisions. As much as Stephen uplifted his team, I have witnessed other new leaders undermine the spirit and capability of teams and ultimately the success of their organisations. These impacts are not limited to those in leadership roles; even one new member of a team can enable or detract from the success of the group.

Adopting a strategic approach

Developing the capabilities needed now and in the future is an important strategic priority for any business. Recruitment plays an essential role in enabling you to acquire the knowledge, skills, experience and behaviours required to achieve both immediate and longer-term goals. Too many managers treat recruitment as an operational process, however, simply reacting to the need to fill a new or recently vacated position as it arises. Often these managers adopt an approach that is not planned or even considered, which inevitably leads to challenges in finding or selecting the right people when they need them. Too often I observe these managers, eager to fill the role, compromise and make hiring decisions that ultimately lead to performance, engagement or behavioural issues down the line.

Being strategic in your approach requires that you take steps that enable you to find and recruit the right people for your business long before you need them. Establishing a reputation for being an employer of choice and developing a pool of talented internal and external candidates are important strategic priorities. In other words, not only should you develop a pool of candidates to tap into as required, but you should also influence these candidates' desire to work for you.

Just as important are the strategies you employ to find candidates when they aren't already known to you. Ideally you will have people waiting in the wings, but when you don't, how you go about searching for candidates is crucial to success. At times the best way to do that is to work in partnership with recruitment consultants. Getting the most from these relationships takes a focused and deliberate approach that we will explore later in this chapter. Once you have found potential candidates, then the priority shifts to ensuring you make the right decisions and persuading candidates to sign up for the opportunity.

In the sections ahead we will explore these strategic priorities and the steps you can take to ensure your approach is planned and ultimately successful.

Developing talent pools

Intensifying competition for talent and the increasingly global nature of that competition is driving a growing need for organisations to proactively develop a pool of talent from which they can draw candidates. While millions of people are unemployed, unfortunately this does not always mean the capabilities your business needs are readily available. Finding quality candidates is increasingly the real challenge. As baby boomers leave the workforce, knowledge and skills will also be retired, and the workforce in many countries is expected to steadily decline over the decades ahead. These demographic changes will inevitably impact on the availability of a diverse talent pool from which employers can recruit.

Leading HR outsourcing organisation Talent2 defines a talent pool as 'a community of qualified internal and external candidates who are actively interested in your organisation, your industry and your success and are engaged over time to fill vacancies and refer people they know'. Building talent pools is a necessity to create and sustain competitive advantage. Smart organisations are already building and executing the relevant strategies required, ensuring they take a measured and proactive approach to engaging with their current and future talent.

The most important steps to adopting a talent pool strategy include the following:

☑ *Consider and plan for the future.* Define what talent you will need in the foreseeable future. Understand the outcomes you are looking to achieve and the tasks that need to be undertaken to make them happen. What capabilities are needed to complete these tasks?

☑ *Understand the talent landscape.* Where is this talent now? How many people are already in your business versus working for somebody else or themselves?

☑ *Consider your options.* How can you access the talent needed? For example, do you need to hire permanent staff or is there an end date, which means you would be better served by engaging casuals, contractors or consultants?

☑ *Prioritise internal recruitment.* Adopt a 'grow-your-own' philosophy and strategy that sees you invest in the development of the people you already have on your team, keeping them with your business.

☑ *Manage your relationships with external candidates.* Once you start attracting people to your business you need to be ready for them. It's time to start regularly engaging with them. The advent of social media is dramatically changing the way you can stay in touch with people who are interested in working for your business in the future.

☑ *Take an annual view.* Every year take the time to project what skill sets you will need based on predictable attrition and business strategy.

Growing an internal pool of talent

Recruitment is not just about hiring people from outside your organisation. Adopting a 'grow-your-own' strategy is a powerful way of building a pool of talent within your own business that you can recruit from. By providing your team with exciting development and career opportunities, not only can you access the talent you need but you also improve your ability to retain talented people.

Be disciplined, patient, supportive and creative in finding ways to develop and promote talented and committed staff. Focus on developing leadership, management and role-specific competencies internally, and whenever possible promote your staff into more senior positions before searching for external candidates. Remember, however, that it is not always possible to recruit from within. While a grow-your-own strategy is an important priority, never compromise the quality of your hiring decisions. Appointing someone to a role for which they are neither suited nor qualified can have a devastating impact not only on your team's success but also on that individual's career and confidence.

In particular, be careful when considering promoting high-performing staff into management positions. Time and again I have seen organisations appoint their most successful team member into a management role when they are far from the best person for the job. The capabilities and attributes required of a successful manager are vastly different from those typically required of someone in an individual contributor position. If your team member is performing highly in their current role, this does not mean they are necessarily qualified or suited to leading others.

Developing external talent pools

It's wise to remember that in any external recruitment process there is an element of both 'buying' capability into your business and 'selling' what you offer. Talented candidates who understand their value in the market are typically assessing you as much as you are evaluating them. Building a pool of quality external candidates means proactively and consistently fostering interest in working for your business and team. The goal is to build a pool of people eager to explore opportunities within your organisation when they arise.

To promote your business, first you need to understand what you offer — that is, your employment value proposition (EVP). It's crucial that you are able to articulate the benefits of joining your team. Reflect on the things you provide your employees, such as career or development opportunities, your culture and your approach to leadership. Are there financial incentives or rewards that set you apart? Do you offer benefits that allow your team to balance the demands of work and life? Fundamentally, you need to understand how attractive your organisation is to the talent you want to attract and then tell them about it.

Regardless of how you choose to present your organisation to the external world, the most important driver of your reputation is what your current and past team members choose to say about you. Don't underestimate the power of their influence, and focus your efforts on providing an employment experience that is worth promoting. Inspire your staff to speak positively about what it's like working for you. To the extent that it's possible, work to ensure that when you part ways with members of your team you maintain a healthy relationship. Treating people with respect and consideration, irrespective of the circumstances of their departure, will go some way to influencing their willingness to speak positively about your business after they have moved on. Don't hesitate to ask your staff to promote your business proactively; if they are proud of working for you they will do so gladly.

There are many ways you can spread the word and build a strong reputation for being an employer of choice, including through:

- talking to prospective employees in your networks, and at seminars and conferences

- building relationships with recruitment consultants willing and able to promote your business

- soliciting for media mentions and articles that showcase your culture or team successes

- investing thought and energy into building your 'career page' on your website.

Often organisations fail to leverage their efforts to attract people effectively—for example, when approached by candidates of high potential or interviewing more than one suitable person for a role. Their biggest mistake is failing to keep track of these people, making it difficult to contact them when a suitable opportunity arises. When you believe a candidate is worth considering further, keep a record of your assessment and any roles you think they may be suitable for down the track. Let these people know you are interested in staying in touch and encourage them to do the same.

Ways you can keep the lines of communication open include sharing news through newsletters or blogs, using online tools such as LinkedIn, Facebook or Twitter to stay in touch, and even meeting with those with whom you would like to foster a relationship. The most important starting point is choosing to take a proactive approach to maintaining a connection with those you have worked hard to attract in the first place.

Planning to succeed

Quality outcomes are underpinned by a well-considered and well-planned approach. A common mistake managers make is to launch into a recruitment process without first giving enough thought to what they want to achieve or how to go about it. This is among the most common reasons I observe for poor hiring decisions that ultimately lead to substandard performance, unsuccessful behaviour and turnover in a role.

Before getting started it's crucial that you have a clear view of the candidate you are looking for. This includes distinguishing between the 'non-negotiable' capabilities they must bring and those that would be 'nice to have'. Just as important is having a good understanding of what it will take for the right person to fit in with the rest of the team. Later we will explore how to develop selection criteria that will guide your search and assessment of each candidate throughout your entire recruitment process.

Documenting the role and your selection criteria in a position description (PD) at the start of your process is crucial to success. It's not the document itself that matters; real value comes from the thought process you go through and the clarity that results. A well-developed PD will help everyone involved in the process keep focused on what and who you are looking for. It can also be leveraged to provide applicants with a clear picture of the role on offer and what you are looking for from the successful candidate.

Priority 1: design the role

To attract and retain quality candidates first you need to make sure the job is designed well. Creating a role with various responsibilities that demand capabilities, attributes and preferences that are vastly different from one another can make finding suitable candidates extremely difficult. For example, a role that requires a candidate to have strong strategic capabilities and yet most of the time perform highly operational functions is likely to be difficult to fill. When designing roles, consider each of the elements included in priorities 2 and 3. Be pragmatic about the type of candidate needed and the likelihood of success in finding that person.

Priority 2: understand the role

Create an inventory of the most important things you need to understand and be able to articulate about any role for which you are recruiting. Such a blueprint, which will help you not only to select the right person but also to establish clear performance expectations once they join, should include the following:

- primary objective (what the role is there to achieve and how success is defined)

- scope of responsibility and accountability

- level of direction given and autonomy permitted

- key tasks regularly performed

- standard of performance expected

- complexity and challenges anticipated

- important relationships (the people the role often collaborates or interacts with, including colleagues, clients, managers or service providers).

Priority 3: determine who will be the best person for the job

The next step is to develop a profile of the person most likely to succeed. Develop selection criteria focused on both essential requirements and those on which you can afford to be flexible. Include not only the capabilities the best person will need but also the approach they must adopt. Make sure you understand the required:

- *knowledge and skills:* What are the minimum requirements for a candidate to be considered? Consider technical, organisational and interpersonal capabilities. For example, do they need to be able to establish plans, organise processes and people, impart information, persuade or influence others, or deal with challenging personalities or conflict?

- *experience:* What scenarios or environments must they have experienced before and performed well in?

- *qualifications:* What is required or what is preferred (for example, a degree, trade certificate, licence)?

- *values and behaviours:* What must they bring in order to fit your culture?

Priority 4: decide what your assessment process will involve

Before you start to search the market be ready to explain to applicants the process you are asking them to participate in. When deciding what steps to include, ensure you allow for a thorough assessment while avoiding an excessively onerous process that may deter some high-quality candidates from applying. While it may be tempting to take short cuts, in most circumstances it is important to have interviewed the successful candidate more than once. Ideally those who are shortlisted from the first interview will be invited to attend a second.

While planning is important, so too is flexibility. Wherever possible, work broadly within the process you establish but be prepared to adapt your approach when needed. You and your candidates will need to know:

- the format of interviews (individual or group)
- the number of interviews the successful candidate is likely to be expected to attend
- whether you will use assessment tools such as psychometrics, abilities tests or assessment centres, or written assignments such as case studies or presentations
- acceptable referees for reference checks and the person who will talk to them.

Priority 5: establish the selection panel

It's important to decide upfront who will be involved in the process and in what capacity. Identify those who will share their opinions to support your decision and those who will actively participate in the selection of the successful candidate. Decide who will participate in interviews or any other assessment processes you adopt and the role you need them to play.

Priority 6: *determine how you will go about finding suitable candidates*

Consider first whether or not you already know potential candidates within your internal or external talent pools. If you do, is a broader search necessary or are you confident you can progress immediately to formally assessing them? If a candidate search is necessary, what avenues will you take? Refer to the next section for further insight into finding suitable candidates outside of your organisation.

Finding external candidates

In this section we will explore how to optimise your ability to attract quality applicants for the role. We will look at how to design effective job advertisements, encourage staff and colleagues to refer candidates, and get the most from working with recruitment consultants.

Option 1: *encourage staff referrals*

One of the most effective ways of finding candidates is by encouraging your staff and colleagues to refer people. Often they will already know quality candidates, whether they are colleagues from previous workplaces, people they have met at seminars and conferences, friends, friends of friends or candidates they have met through other recruitment processes.

Tap into this network by asking your team to refer those they believe meet the requirements of the role and fit the culture of the business. Most people will avoid recommending candidates they are not confident meet the brief. While not always the case, most people are careful about who they recommend out of concern for how the person will reflect on them.

Offering to pay staff who recommended candidates who successfully complete the first six months of employment can be an effective way of incentivising people to contribute. This is typically a more cost-effective approach to sourcing candidates than engaging the services of a recruitment consultant.

Option 2: tap into networks

Reflect on your own network and whether you know people who can recommend candidates. Ask your colleagues to consider their networks and who they know who may be able to help in the search process. Sometimes you may know someone who knows someone who can recommend people worth approaching. Potential candidates may know, or be known by, past employees, industry colleagues or consultants. Referrals may also come from your clients, service providers and partners. For example, do you or someone in your network know outplacement agents and career transition specialists working with candidates looking for a new direction or job? Some of these people have been made redundant despite being qualified high performers and are worth finding.

Option 3: advertise

If your networks have yielded little or no return, it may be time to consider advertising. When deciding where to advertise, consider which forum or medium is likely to have the greatest impact in attracting the type of people you are looking for. Keep in mind that often the best candidates are not actively searching for a new job and may not see your advertisement placed on a job board or in the career section of a newspaper. Options you should consider include:

- promoting the role through industry journals or professional associations

- online job boards such as www.seek.com.au or www.monster .com, which are typically cost effective and convenient to use

- newspapers, which, while often costly, can add value, particularly for senior management vacancies

- your company website, particularly if you have a strong employer reputation and people are likely to visit your site for career opportunities

- your company newsletter or other regular publications you may produce and share with an audience outside your business

- social media and networking sites such as LinkedIn, Facebook and Twitter, which are fast gaining momentum as effective ways of finding candidates.

An effective advertisement will attract not only more applicants but also the right type of candidate. A well-written and -formatted advertisement is easier to read, making it more likely a job seeker will understand the role, their suitability and how it may fit with what they are looking for, including their career aspirations and lifestyle preferences.

To write an effective job advertisement that achieves its objectives, ensure you:

- include relevant and informative content

- first list the things most important to you and most appealing to candidates

- present information in a logical order and use subheadings to break up the content

- use bullet-point lists to keep the word count down and make the detail easy to scan

- provide enough information without being verbose.

You should always include the:

- primary objective of the role

- work environment and culture of the company

- essential skills, experience and qualifications needed

- opportunities the role or business will offer the successful candidate

- location (not everyone is willing to travel or relocate, and it is better to eliminate these candidates upfront).

Option 4: work with recruitment consultants

Engaging a recruiter to help you source and attract candidates can be an effective solution, particularly when you have neither the time nor the expertise to manage the process directly. Often this can be a relatively costly option, with success highly dependent on the capabilities of the agency and recruitment consultant engaged. How well you work with recruiters profoundly influences the likelihood of success. Included later in this chapter is a comprehensive guide to getting the best possible service and value for your money.

Candidate assessment

A common mistake managers make is to place too strong a focus on a candidate's technical knowledge, skills and experience. Some underestimate the value and importance of ensuring that the people they hire are a culture fit, are motivated and have career aspirations aligned with the direction or future needs of the business. Others may hire the 'best of a bad bunch' when they find it hard to attract quality candidates or the position needs to be filled quickly.

Managing the process well

In this section we will explore how to facilitate the assessment process, accurately assess each candidate and ultimately make the best hiring decisions.

Priority 1: understand the 'buy and sell' equation

Recruitment is a two-way street; not only are you looking for the best candidate, but they are looking for the best job and employer. Leverage the process to promote the benefits of the role and working for your business while being careful not to exaggerate or over-promise. There is no point pursuing someone to join your team if they are likely to be disappointed or unprepared to tackle the challenges involved.

Priority 2: keep the process moving quickly

Being thorough is important, but keep in mind that an unreasonably lengthy or stalled process can lead to quality candidates pursuing other options or losing interest. Don't compromise the process by taking short cuts, but endeavour to move forward quickly and keep candidates informed.

Priority 3: use psychometric tools wisely

Psychometric tools can help you assess candidates but remember they are indicative, not predictive. Use them for guidance rather than as a stand-alone decision-making tool; information gleaned should be used to design interview questions and guide conversations with referees.

Priority 4: document

Keep notes to help you accurately recall your assessment of each candidate; this will be important when comparing the people you have met and selecting the best person for the job. Equally, it will ensure you are able to demonstrate why you reached the decision you did if challenged by an unsuccessful candidate on the grounds of lawful compliance.

Priority 5: leverage your recruitment panel

Immediately following each interview take the time to discuss the extent to which you and other interviewers believe the candidate fits your selection criteria. When you have interviewed all candidates reconvene to compare each against the other and discuss the best way to move forward.

Assessing culture fit

While it can be tempting to hire the person with the most experience or impressive technical qualifications, never compromise the importance you place on cultural alignment with your business.

Never hire someone if you are not confident they will bring values and behaviours that fit with your culture. Assess how aligned every candidate's approach to doing their job and being a member of your team is with the way you want people to behave in your workplace.

Time and again I have observed leaders make the fatal mistake of hiring people based on their technical capabilities or experience while ignoring clear signals of culture misfit. I have yet to see such decisions turn out well. Without exception the appointed candidate leaves the organisation soon after joining, becomes a disruptive or destructive influence, or performs poorly.

In chapter 3 I introduced three core values that in my experience matter most to the success of any individual, team or organisation: behaviours that reflect trust, respect and personal accountability will underpin the quality of any hiring decision you make. While there is no way of predicting exactly how people will behave, there are things you can do to maximise your chances of getting it right.

Here are the most important things you should do to assess the culture fit of every candidate:

☑ Identify the values and behaviours you want to assess and ask questions that expose the candidate's alignment with each.

☑ Read between the lines and observe attitude when reading application documents, conducting interviews or completing reference checks.

☑ Assess the candidate's priorities, philosophies, beliefs, prejudices and motivations. Consider the likely impact each will have on their approach to doing their job and dealing with others.

(continued)

☑ Observe how they engage with you and other people before, during and after interviews and other face-to-face interactions.

☑ Notice shifts in behaviour or expressions of attitude towards individuals and groups. For example, does the candidate respond differently to people they perceive to be senior, level or junior to them?

Assessing competence

Being competent takes more than having knowledge, skills and experience; it's our ability to effectively apply these capabilities that ultimately determines success. As we explored in the introduction to this book, it is critical to ensure that the people you hire bring both talent and behaviours that allow their effective application. No matter how qualified or experienced a candidate is, keep in mind and assess the potential for them to lack common sense or struggle to work well with others. Consider the extent to which they are likely to apply their capabilities consistently, particularly in the circumstances unique to the role you have on offer.

In an ideal world every person you hire will have the competencies needed on day one. However, often even strong candidates will only partially meet your selection criteria. Understanding which capabilities are non-negotiable and which are 'nice to have' is an important starting point. Then you need to consider whether or not you have the time and resources to provide any training or development needed. Before making your hiring decision understand which is more important—their ability to learn or their capacity to immediately 'hit the ground running'.

Assessing competence shouldn't be limited to the individual you are considering hiring. It's important to consider the capabilities of your whole team and understand how this candidate needs to fit in. Do their capabilities need to complement or supplement those already available? Are you looking to strengthen the group's abilities in specific areas or are you simply searching for someone who can do the same things other team members can also do?

To assess competence, look for evidence that the candidate has:

- the ability to apply their capabilities consistently within the context of the role

- an awareness of the core objectives, responsibilities, challenges and complexities of the role

- the levels of knowledge, skill and experience needed to perform at the standard expected

- the ability to plan and integrate a number of different tasks to achieve an outcome

- the ability to respond to irregularities, breakdowns and other unanticipated events

- the capacity to deal with the responsibilities and expectations of the work environment, including working with others.

Assessing role fit

The characteristics of a role with the same job title are likely to vary from one organisation to another. For example, an HR manager in one business may spend most of their time focused on policy interpretation and process coordination, while in another organisation development and talent management may be important priorities. The type of candidate suited to each of these roles is vastly different.

It's important to assess the extent to which the core functions and requirements of the position match not only what the candidate is capable of doing, but also what they are looking for in a job. Important considerations include the following:

- Will the role provide enough reward and challenge to ensure job satisfaction? If yes, for how long? Does this suit your requirements?

- Do most tasks and responsibilities align with the candidate's work preferences?

- Do their skills and attributes (such as their communication style) suit the job?

- Is it likely that the candidate will be motivated to grow with the role over time?

Assessing career fit

How often have you hired someone only to have them leave a short time later because a better offer came along? Have you engaged the services of someone only to have them work to elevate their role beyond the scope of responsibilities for which they were hired? To keep talented people with your business and engaged with their role for any reasonable period of time, make sure the job you have to offer is aligned with their career aspirations.

Take, for example, the client service supervisor looking to become a manager. They may well accept your offer of another position as supervisor; however, they are also highly likely to leave if a management role somewhere else comes along. Offering anyone looking for advancement a job that has them performing tasks they believe they have already mastered is risky.

If keeping people for the long term is important, then consider also how likely it is that you will be able to offer them a step-up in their career beyond the role you are hiring for now. Of course aspirations change, but understanding what the candidate wants to be doing down the track will give you some sense of whether or not those plans fit with the future direction and priorities of your business.

To assess career fit effectively, make sure you understand the candidate's:

- ideal next role

- longer-term aspirations and time horizon

- drive and determination to achieve their aspirations
- self-perceptions and beliefs about their ability to advance as intended.

Conducting effective interviews

Interviews are an important opportunity for you and your candidates to get to know one another and assess the extent to which the role is the right next step for them. The value you get from any interview comes down to how prepared you are and how well you facilitate the meeting. Too many managers choose to 'wing it' and fail to fully leverage the benefits of an interview.

Planning and preparation

Here are the most important things you can do to avoid that approach.

Priority 1: prepare an interview guide for each round

A well-structured interview guide includes questions you will ask and a rating scale to assess the quality of responses you receive. The most useful questions are those that ask for examples of when the candidate has performed a task, assumed a responsibility, confronted a challenge or achieved an outcome. Asking candidates to reflect on past experiences allows you to assess the depth of their competence and observe the attitudes and behaviours they brought to each situation.

Priority 2: select and secure an appropriate venue

Make sure you have a confidential and comfortable setting in which to conduct interviews. A public venue such as a café may be distracting or uncomfortable for your candidate. It's important also to protect the candidate's right to confidentiality, so select a private venue where no-one walking by would be able to observe or overhear your conversation.

Priority 3: coordination

It's important to know before you begin who will be responsible for what. If there is more than one person interviewing, what role will you each play? Who will lead? Who will ask the questions? Just as important is making sure everyone on the selection panel has a copy of the candidate's CV as well as the interview guide. Inform everyone well in advance of the time and venue for each interview.

Priority 4: preparation on the day

Refresh your memory before greeting the candidate. Using the wrong name or being unaware of which role they have applied for is not a good start to the process. Take the time to review their application and remind yourself why you invited them to attend the interview. Make a note of anything you are unclear about or on which you would like additional information to ensure you explore these areas adequately.

Facilitation

The way in which you facilitate an interview will affect your ability to accurately assess each candidate and positively influence their perceptions. Included in this section are the most important things you must do to leverage the benefit of each interview.

Priority 1: put candidates at ease

An interview should never be conducted as an interrogation or be overly rigid. It is far more effective to have a conversation with your candidates. Avoid adopting an excessively formal style; rather, conduct interviews in a way that encourages people to relax and speak freely. By doing so you are far more likely to see who they really are and be able to assess the extent to which they are suitable.

Encourage candidates to let you know if they are unsure what you are asking and assure them it is not your intention to try to 'catch them out'. Explain that the purpose of the interview is to help you understand their ability to perform the role, as well as what they are looking for next in their career. Let them know that you understand they too are assessing the opportunity and that you are happy to answer any questions they have about the role or your organisation.

Priority 2: be flexible

While it is important to follow your interview guide, you should also be flexible and allow the process to flow. Ask unplanned questions when a candidate's response doesn't tell you everything you need to know or creates a perception that you are eager to validate. Keep in mind that candidates may not always understand what you are asking, so it may be necessary to rephrase some questions.

Priority 3: interview etiquette

Applying professional standards of conduct will go a long way to ensuring you conduct interviews not only effectively but also appropriately.

Here are the most important things to do or avoid in the interview:

☑ Be polite and friendly.

☑ Thank the candidate for their time and interest in the role.

☑ Maintain eye contact and demonstrate interest in what they are saying.

☑ Be conversational but make sure you are listening more than talking.

☑ Avoid interrupting unless the candidate is being overly verbose.

(continued)

☑ Never argue—candidates aren't there to hear your opinions.

☑ Don't ask personal questions that may be interpreted as inappropriate or discriminatory.

☑ Avoid comments that may make a candidate feel uncomfortable.

☑ Avoid forming a fixed view based on your first impressions; give candidates a reasonable opportunity to make their case. However, if your gut instinct persists in ringing warning bells, listen and explore why!

Priority 4: explain what will happen next

At the end of an interview it is important to let candidates know when they are likely to hear from you again and what the next steps are likely to be. Keep in mind that your preferred candidate(s) may be considering other roles and the timing of your process could bear on their commitment and interest. Whether or not you have a favourable impression of the candidate it is a matter of professional courtesy that you keep them well informed.

Getting the best from recruitment consultants

It is crucial to select and work with the recruitment consultants who best suit your needs.

Priority 1: select the right agency

Skilled and committed recruitment consultants demonstrate interest in understanding your business and the role you want to fill. They adopt a strategic and proactive approach and work hard to influence your preferred candidate's decision to join your team. In contrast, some simply play a numbers game and rely on their process to connect employers and candidates, with limited value added. The best recruiters are skilled at assessing candidates, understand your business and are well positioned to find qualified people through their extensive networks. Those who rely heavily on their database or responses to job advertisements are unlikely to perform well.

Priority 2: build your relationship and work in partnership

As in any relationship, success is influenced by the commitment of both parties. Support your recruitment partners to succeed by giving them the time and information they need. Help them to understand your business and the role they are hiring for. Provide constructive feedback along the way to enable them to adapt and finetune their approach until a good result is achieved. It's important to understand that there must be mutual benefit and respect in the relationship or they are unlikely to be motivated to work hard for you. It is typically more effective to retain a single agency to manage an assignment, but if you do choose to brief multiple agencies make sure you are upfront and honest with everyone about that.

Priority 3: value advice

To leverage maximum value, expect and allow your recruitment partners to provide more than a résumé referral service. Invite and listen to the advice they offer about both the approach taken and the candidates presented for consideration. If you have chosen the right consultant, allow them to earn your trust and put faith in their advice. Remember that a skilled recruitment consultant can add value throughout the process including sourcing strategies, candidate assessment and negotiations.

Priority 4: dedicate the time needed

More often than not you will want to fill a role in the shortest possible time, but speed should not be the focus of your recruiter's approach. It is important to be reasonable in your expectations and allow recruiters the time they need to do the best possible job for you. Of course that is not to suggest you shouldn't encourage a sense of urgency, but be careful not to compromise the quality of the process by demanding that specific time frames be met. Keep in mind that it can take a few weeks before you see a shortlist, especially if you use a good-quality service that includes sourcing and screening applications, interviewing candidates and obtaining reference checks.

Priority 5: expect drive and commitment

The best candidates don't remain on recruitment databases for long, regardless of how competitive the job market is. Attracting great candidates will often take more than a passive or reactive approach. Securing them will often involve competing with other organisations. Ensure that the recruiters you work with are committed to an active search process and able to sell the benefits of working for your business.

Priority 6: candidate care

Whether or not they are the best person for the role, every candidate deserves to be treated with respect and courtesy. Ensure the approach adopted by consultants working on your behalf is considerate, ethical and professional. Keep in mind that their approach reflects on you and your organisation's culture.

In summary, to optimise the return on your investment in hiring recruitment consultants it's important to set clear expectations and hold them accountable to acceptable standards of performance. Important measures of a recruiter's success are:

- an open and honest approach

- high standards of candidate care

- the recommendation of quality candidates that meet your selection criteria

- a demonstrated commitment to placing the best possible candidate for every role

- a thorough understanding of your business, culture and the role you are looking to fill

- an intimate understanding of the market and where to find quality candidates

- the delivery of time- and cost-effective recruitment solutions.

Chapter summary: the most important things to do and avoid

Must-do checklist

The most important things you must do to achieve your recruitment objectives are to:

✓ adopt a planned and strategic approach

✓ grow your own: develop people already on your team and look for opportunities to promote them

✓ proactively build external pools of talent

✓ leverage your networks to find the best people

✓ select candidates based on competence, culture fit, and career and role fit

✓ ensure candidates have an accurate view of the role and what they are signing up for.

Common mistakes to avoid

The most common mistakes I observe people managers make that undermine their ability to successfully recruit include:

✗ launching into a recruitment process before knowing what and who they are looking for

(continued)

Chapter summary (cont'd)

✗ failing to take the steps necessary to allow them to accurately assess each candidate

✗ compromising on culture fit because a candidate has the skills or experience they are looking for

✗ being closed-minded to some candidates who don't immediately fit their rigid view of the best person for the role.

Chapter 5

Communication

Once again I saw that unfiltered, face-to-face communication is the key to many of the world's problems. It's the key to conflict resolution and leads to hope for the future. Words can change ideas, bring peace or war — or foment a revolution.

Richard Branson, founder and Chairman of Virgin Group
and author of *Screw Business As Usual* (2011)

It's unlikely to come as a surprise to many people in business to hear that communication matters to success. I have witnessed the impact of both great and poor communication on the strength of relationships and the effectiveness of people at work. How well we communicate has the potential to influence awareness, understanding, trust, respect and engagement with others, and ultimately their willingness to interact, let alone collaborate.

Throughout this book communication emerges as a critical enabler of all of the tools in the people manager's toolkit. In this chapter we will look at how you can leverage communication to influence both the spirit and the performance of your team. Inspiring your team to strive for great results and enabling effective application of systems and processes are examples of why a strategic approach to communication is a critical priority for any manager of people.

In this chapter we will explore:

- planning what, when and how you communicate to optimise positive effect
- the importance of balancing telling, asking and listening
- inspiring commitment and engagement by targeting communications to your audience
- questioning and challenging to reach the best decisions and outcomes
- how being clear, concise and timely influences success.

Achieving a consistently high standard of effective communication across your business means first recognising it as important and then making it an ongoing priority. Being deliberate and specific about the outcomes you are working to achieve through your communication efforts goes a long way to helping you to realise them. People need to understand not only how senior management, HR, head office or 'corporate' are responsible for effective communication but also what is expected from every manager and team member.

In this chapter I will share with you the things that, in my experience, have the greatest impact on the value and benefit of communication in organisations of all sizes across any industry. We don't, however, have room for an in-depth look at the success of communication exchanges between individuals; neither will we explore communication topics such as mediation and conflict resolution. Although critical capabilities of any people manager, they fall outside the scope of this book.

What success looks like

The effectiveness of communication strategies and practices can be measured by observing the behaviour of managers and how people feel about working for the business. Included here are examples of these and other outcome measures of good communication.

In organisations that practise effective communication, managers:

- provide regular and up-to-date information about objectives, strategies, priorities and progress
- communicate the potential and actual consequences of decisions
- proactively influence awareness and understanding
- leverage the full potential of the team by listening to their ideas and insights
- provide honest and constructive feedback with respect and sensitivity.

In organisations that practise effective communication, team members:

- are appropriately informed, particularly about matters that affect them
- identify communication as a strength of their manager and the business
- feel considered and consulted
- never feel misinformed
- are willing to share and discuss information with their colleagues.

Outcomes

- Well-informed decisions are made.
- Communications foster healthy working relationships.
- Strategies and approaches have a positive impact on culture and engagement.
- People are given the opportunity to ask questions and receive considered responses.
- Good communications enable important outcomes.

Case study
Dancing in the dark

At an industry conference a number of years ago I met John, a finance manager for a large utilities business who was trying to drive change through his department. John shared with me the frustrations he had with his boss, Phillip, whom he found unapproachable, secretive and resistant to change. John asked me to help him engage with Phillip and get him to understand what the team needed from him, which included a clearer vision and strategic plan for their department.

Phillip spent long hours meeting with consultants or locked away in his office. As a result he remained largely a mystery to John, who struggled to gain enough access to him. John and the rest of the team were cautious about what Phillip was working on, with some fearing he was hatching a plan to outsource their jobs. The list of assumptions made about Phillip was long and varied; what was consistent across the team was that no-one understood what Phillip was doing or why he believed it was important.

Phillip was also reported to be guilty of a myriad other management sins including lacking compassion, trust, appreciation or respect for members of the team. Phillip could be aloof and remote and failed to demonstrate that he valued the contributions of team members. He also failed to set clear expectations and when disappointed with performance he struggled to communicate what needed to improve.

John was reluctant to challenge Phillip, so we agreed that I would consult directly to Phillip and work to influence his awareness and support for change. I soon learned that Phillip did indeed have a vision and strategy and had spent many hours developing an impressive plan with the support of consultants. Phillip could present a bound document detailing every aspect of his view of their future. What he clearly had failed to do, however, was consult with and engage his team. At no point in the planning process had

Phillip asked his managers, let alone team members, for their input; he reached isolated decisions and then didn't tell anyone about them.

Working closely with Phillip over time it became evident to me that poor communication was driving many of the perceptions held of him and the challenges he faced. Phillip cared far more than people thought and reflected more deeply than people assumed. The problem was he never told anyone; he was too busy with his head down working in his own bubble to let people see and influence his thought processes, too busy to stop and be polite, to connect with people and demonstrate interest. Phillip's colleagues perceived Phillip as being all talk and no action. He spent a lot of time talking to business stakeholders about his plans for the future, but he rarely spoke about what his team was currently achieving and how they were already adding value.

Phillip's story offers a prime example of the far-reaching consequences of poor communication. But the reason I have included it here is because there is a happy ending. Phillip took responsibility for the challenges he faced and worked hard to shift his approach and build stronger relationships with his team and clients. He realised that in order to be successful in his current role, and also in his future career, he needed to improve his communication skills significantly. Over the 18 months that I worked with Phillip and his team I witnessed a dramatic change in both his communication style and its effect on his performance. Phillip went from being an essentially shy and reserved manager who presented as aloof and disconnected to being actively engaged in discussing issues and exploring ideas with his team. He was still not the greatest motivational speaker, but by using sound and logical reasoning he was able to share a compelling vision for the future that inspired increased commitment from many people on the team. It was rewarding to observe the confidence Phillip exuded in all of his interactions with his team. The ability to communicate more effectively with his group had a clear and visible impact on Phillip's strength of leadership, presence and happiness.

Adopting a strategic approach

Of course spontaneity shouldn't be staged, but the approach managers are expected to adopt and the communication strategies they are expected to implement should be well understood and consistently applied. Deploying a strategic approach means planning, with every manager implementing those plans in a disciplined way.

Plans must be targeted to specific outcomes. For example, businesses committed to building the spirit of their team should expect managers to communicate in a way any reasonable person would consider fair, respectful, honest and sensitive. Organisations looking to build a more collaborative team culture should ask managers to encourage open discussion and healthy yet robust debate among their staff.

While it isn't always possible to plan communications, even when you have only moments to convey a message it should be considered. Understanding the key objectives and principles that underpin the organisation's approach to communications is a valuable tool to guide every manager in those moments.

Planning to succeed

Often I work with managers who are surprised to learn that their teams are looking for more and improved communication. Just as common are individuals or groups who feel they have been misinformed or are 'out of the loop' despite the business's belief that it has communicated effectively. As George Bernard Shaw once said, 'The single biggest problem in communication is the illusion that it has taken place'. The vast majority of staff surveys I have facilitated have revealed a perception that communication can improve in one way or another.

No matter how well you communicate there are likely to be those in your team who want more information or a greater opportunity to contribute their opinions or ideas. A planned and targeted approach will keep your efforts focused and purposeful while avoiding simply reacting to individual perceptions and wants. It is essential to remain open to your team's feedback, but you must also remain focused and strategic in your approach. Through the rest of this chapter we will explore the most important strategies and approaches to enabling a consistently high standard of communication.

Planning to communicate well requires that you understand what you need to communicate to whom for what reasons, the sensitivities you need to manage and the timing that will be most effective. Table 5.1 provides examples of the parameters to consider while planning your communication efforts. These parameters will be explored throughout this chapter.

Table 5.1: parameters to consider while planning your communication

Why	Inform	Consult	Educate	Inspire
What	Decisions; actions and priorities	Advice or insight	Anticipated events	Circumstances
Who	Individuals	Groups	Interested parties	Stakeholders
Timing	Immediate	Planned future date	Unknown	Ongoing
Medium	Written	In person	Phone	Video
Forum	Formal setting	Casual setting	Public	Private
Frequency	As required	Intermittent	Regular	For a defined period
Sensitivity	None known	Discomfort likely	Highly sensitive	Potentially volatile

Critical objectives

Communication is integral to everything we do in business and a key driver of staff retention and engagement. In this section we will explore essential communication objectives that strengthen your ability to leverage your team's full potential. These include earning buy-in and ensuring that people are informed, and that you consult with them to draw on their ideas and insights. Each objective is equally important; each supports your ability to foster healthy relationships with your team and utilise what they know to enable the best possible decisions and results.

Often managers express frustration with the 'delays' caused by the need for staff communication. These managers are frequently responsible for driving significant change or are simply tired of the day-to-day demands of leading a team. They fail to place a high priority on communicating with their team either to earn their support or to access their knowledge and ideas. Many I observe don't even bother to take the time to pass on vital information their team need.

Communication is a non-negotiable priority for every people manager. Unless communication is managed well, your ability to effectively apply any of the other tools in the people manager's toolkit is diminished. Benefits of adopting a strategic approach to communication include the following:

- People will have the information and understanding they need to do their jobs well.

- You will be able to leverage your team's collective wisdom to develop and implement robust plans.

- People can share their insights and experiences, allowing them to contribute at a level that reflects their potential rather than their position.

- Your team's spirit will be energised because each member's sense of personal value, purpose and meaning is enhanced.

- You will earn respect and loyalty from your team.

Keeping people informed and consulted

How much people feel they are informed and consulted can significantly influence the degree to which they feel trusted or respected. Our spirit is unquestionably energised by the trust and respect we feel when we are privy to important information or are asked to contribute our opinions or ideas. All too often, however, I hear people complain that they are not informed of important decisions or included in significant discussions.

It's natural for people, driven by both curiosity and a need for security, to want to know what is going on in their work environment and to have a say in issues that matter to them. As we explored earlier, it can be a challenge to meet the demands and needs of people so they feel appropriately informed and consulted. Listen and be open to suggestions but form your own views about the information or insights people need and the decisions to which they should contribute. Consider what information, insight or input is needed to:

- allow your team to achieve their objectives

- allow people to anticipate what lies ahead

- positively influence the quality of people's working relationships

- enable people to feel comfortable and secure in their role.

Think about what you need to communicate in order to successfully balance honesty and compassion. For example, if there is no purpose or value in sharing information that is likely to unnerve or upset someone, then perhaps it shouldn't be communicated. Be careful, however, not to underestimate the value people attach to knowing the truth or people's capacity for resilience in the face of information that may be disquieting. At times, telling people what may happen can inspire them to dig deep, come together, and battle through difficult or uncertain times and circumstances. The most important thing to do is ensure you balance the truth with equal measures of hope, optimism and sensitivity.

Earning buy-in

Often central to the purpose of communicating with a person or team is building optimism and earning the support needed to turn vision into reality. Typically, people need to believe in what you want them and the team to achieve and why you want to achieve it. They also need to know that they and the team are capable of achieving what you are asking for. When people don't believe ambitious goals are achievable, their efforts are likely to be half-hearted at best. When people 'buy-in', they sign up for the mission because they believe in both the vision and the team's ability to get there. With their buy-in, you are able to tap into their discretionary effort and passionate desire to succeed.

Buy-in simply means earning support for the things you want to do and achieve. Having given their support, your team will more willingly invest time and energy and strive to make it happen. Earning buy-in means influencing the decisions people make about the extent to which they will commit and bring their best effort. Confidence in the merit of a decision or strategy, as well as in the people involved, is a primary driver of a team's buy-in.

Here are the most important communication priorities that support your ability to earn your team's buy-in:

☑ Tell people what underpins your confidence, for example in your vision, priority, strategy or initiative, the team's capabilities or the likelihood of success.

☑ Acknowledge reality — the risks, obstacles and challenges most likely to stand in your way, and how you will overcome them.

☑ Ask people how they want to contribute and wherever possible give them the opportunity to fulfil that role.

☑ Discuss people's hesitations and fears and provide insight or evidence to allay those fears. If there is no certainty, acknowledge that, and reinforce your reasons for hope and confidence.

☑ Demonstrate commitment to continuing to seek and consider the team's insights and ideas.

☑ Provide evidence of how the team's feedback and ideas contribute to decisions, priorities or achievements.

☑ Demonstrate that you value and respect the input and contributions of every member of the team; acknowledge individuals and groups who contribute to achieving the team's goals or model the organisation's values.

Approaching communication well

In this section we will look at four key priorities that underpin an effective approach to communication. These four components apply whether you are communicating with an individual or a group, in writing, over the phone or in person, in a formal or informal setting, or via some other technology-enabled mode of interaction. They may be summarised as behaving well, knowing when you've said enough, balancing telling and listening, and finally questioning and challenging effectively to get the best possible result.

Priority 1: successful behaviour

Communication is among the most significant influencers of the strength of our relationships in any setting. As we explored in chapter 1, trust and respect are the foundations on which any successful relationship is built. The way we communicate influences the respect people have for us and the extent to which they are willing to trust us. In chapter 1 I also shared 10 golden rules of behaviour that most people expect from one another. Each of these behaviours applies as much to communication as to any other tool in the people manager's toolkit. Together they offer a framework to guide our interactions and ensure people perceive our conduct as consistently fair and respectful.

Having and projecting a healthy attitude, and being polite, compassionate and sensitive as well as honest are all essential components of an effective communication approach. The way we communicate influences people's perceptions of us, including our open-mindedness and willingness to acknowledge mistakes or shortcomings, and whether we listen to other people's points of view or learn from their experiences. What and how we communicate also influences how people perceive our accessibility and the extent to which we are connected with our team. Everything we do to communicate directly or indirectly influences our reputation for being capable, approachable, fair, consistent and ultimately trustworthy. These perceptions, in turn, influence how people respond to and engage with us.

Priority 2: know when enough is enough

Teams often provide mixed feedback about the need for both more and less communication. Often what people are asking for is more relevant information, whether about direction, strategy, decisions or performance, and less email traffic or fewer meetings. People want to be communicated with, but they also want to spend as little time as possible away from their work or wading through written correspondence. In other words, while feeling informed and consulted drives employee satisfaction, people are less enthusiastic about investing a lot of time especially if they struggle to see how it adds value. What matters is that you communicate as much as is necessary to ensure every member of your team is on the same page and understands both the expectations of them and how they are performing and fit into the big picture. Avoid communicating too much; that is, to the extent people are likely to 'switch off' or avoid engaging with what you are sharing or asking.

Some people find it hard to open up with their team, their colleagues or even their boss. This is particularly true of reserved, introverted people, who often struggle to let others into their inner world of thoughts and feelings. A common frustration is that such individuals can take people by surprise when their views are suddenly revealed late in a process. Extroverts, on the other hand, are sometimes prone to over-communicate, dominate discussions and share information prematurely. Effective communication lies at the mid point between being reserved and being uninhibited in your approach.

Priority 3: tell, ask and listen

Successful communication demands that we balance the time we spend conveying information to people, asking for their input and listening to their contributions. Often managers focus their communication largely on imparting information about events and priorities or telling people what is ahead and what is expected of them. Staff meetings are frequently limited to business performance updates, new hire introductions and progress reports. One-on-one meetings may focus on the manager's views, with little time dedicated to exploring the individual's perceptions of their own performance. Managers instruct people how to perform their roles and spend limited time exploring the ideas of their team members about how things could be done differently or improved. While keeping people informed and influencing their understanding are critical, so too is asking and listening.

Reflect on how much time you spend asking your team for their opinions or insights. How often do you explore the views of your people? Simply asking is not enough, however; to know that your desire to understand is sincere people need to see you implement at least some of their ideas. Whenever possible if you receive feedback that you don't intend to act on, make sure you communicate why.

Priority 4: question and challenge

How often are you given information that you simply take at face value and apply without question? You know there is another perspective or angle to a problem but don't have the time, resources or even inclination to dig deeper and gather the information you need. Too often in business we rely on information volunteered or presented without questioning and challenging its accuracy or validity. Reflect for a moment on how confident you really are in the information you use every day to do your job. Only when we are willing and able to ask effective questions and challenge information can we get the depth of insight needed to make the best decisions.

Healthy, robust debate in which we question and challenge our colleagues is an essential characteristic of any successful workplace culture. Of course, it is typically unnecessary and certainly impractical to seek to validate every piece of information we consider or apply. However, a commitment to considering different perspectives, challenging conventional wisdom and debating possibilities will provide deeper insight that will be reflected in the quality of the decisions made. To get the best from people, they should never be afraid to speak truthfully and should always be willing to test the ideas and opinions of both their manager and co-workers. Encourage every member of your team to speak out when they doubt or disagree, but also to communicate with respect and sensitivity. Courage and respect together will allow you to create a culture that uses challenging and questioning to achieve the best possible outcomes.

Drivers of a successful communication process

How often do you consider or document the key messages you want to send at a particular time or in a certain forum? Do you think about what key message you want your staff to take away from a meeting, social gathering or written communication? Do you give thought to the words you use to convey your message and what your behaviours say about you? People look for and value vision, commitment and leadership in their manager. The extent to which people appreciate and take comfort from strong leadership is influenced by what and how you and your entire leadership team communicate.

It may not always be necessary to write down the messages you will communicate in any given situation, but it is always crucial to have them clear in your mind. These messages are conveyed not only by what you say but also by how you behave. Keep in mind that not every signal sent or message received is either planned or intentional; our body language, including facial expressions, posture and physical demeanour, speak loudly to people about what we think and how we feel. A challenge for people managers is to learn to control and manage these signals, including those driven by unconscious thoughts and feelings.

Priority 1: be targeted

How often have you been asked questions and found yourself confused as to why you are being consulted? For communication to be effective it must be relevant and purposeful; in other words, both parties need to understand the objective and value of communicating. Simply communicating with more people more often is not the path to success; targeting your communication is a vital ingredient of a successful approach.

Some managers work tirelessly to communicate, yet their teams still tell them they want to be better consulted. Sometimes despite a constant flow of communication people believe the wrong information, focus, timing or even people are involved. What this feedback often indicates is a need for a more targeted approach. For communications to have a positive impact on people they must be relevant to them; they are then far more likely to connect and engage in the process. A targeted approach conveys relevant content for a particular audience at a specific time.

> *Here are the most important things you need to do to ensure a targeted approach:*
>
> ☑ Recognise the purpose of the communication.
>
> ☑ Identify those people who need to be engaged and those who would like to be.

(continued)

☑ Understand the person or group you are communicating with.

☑ Know how your exchange will add value both to them and to you.

☑ Ask, 'Am I the right person to be involved or should I delegate this to someone else?'

☑ Reflect on whether you need to ask, tell or both.

☑ Determine the best medium, setting and time to communicate.

Priority 2: provide clarity

The need to be clear in your communications may seem too obvious a point to make, but think for a moment how often you have found it difficult to understand what someone is trying to say in a document or email. Think of the times you or someone else you have observed misinterpreted the meaning behind someone's words or even their body language? How often have you walked away from a conversation to realise a short time later that you really didn't elicit the information you needed? Providing clarity through your communications can be surprisingly challenging.

Maintaining clarity can be even more frustrating. Messages can become distorted as they are passed from one person or one department to the next. Typically, with no malice intended, people tend to focus on the negative aspects or consequences of the information in question so the message tends to become more pessimistic. Ensuring every member of your team has a clear and consistent understanding of reality requires a planned and disciplined approach to the dissemination of information through your organisation. Managing the way communications flow through your team is an essential priority if you are to achieve consistent clarity.

Here are the most important things you must do to provide communication clarity:

☑ Understand the perception, emotion or understanding you want to influence.

☑ Identify the key messages or elements of information you therefore need to exchange.

☑ Consider the delivery mechanisms that will enable clarity (to avoid distortion of messages).

☑ Avoid big words and complex language that can alienate or confuse.

Priority 3: be concise

Rabbiting on or going the long way about sharing information or asking questions can frustrate and even alienate people. Imparting or gathering information typically needs to be done in the most efficient and resourceful way possible. Communicating concisely is a fundamental skill that enables you to leverage the limited window of opportunity you often have to reach people and hold their attention. If your topic is interesting and you are an engaging communicator, you will have less pressure to be concise. However, some topics simply aren't that interesting and are unlikely to inspire people.

More often than not being concise matters; to help people focus on and absorb what you are saying, make sure you:

☑ limit the number and complexity of the words you use to what is necessary

(continued)

☑ ration the amount of information or the number of key messages you convey in any communication to what your audience is likely to be able to digest

☑ avoid unnecessarily repeating yourself; it's valuable to reinforce key messages but simply saying what you have already said may cause people to 'switch off'

☑ share only information that adds value; background can be valuable, but only when it's relevant to telling the rest of the story

☑ encourage a relaxed and conversational atmosphere, but make sure communication forums don't run over time or people will start to 'switch off'

☑ think about what you are going to say and get it out; speech fillers such as 'um' and 'argh' can be draining and distracting to your listeners

☑ avoid overly wordy lead-ins, especially if you are introducing the person your audience really wants to hear from.

Priority 4: time it well

Timing your communications well starts with understanding who you need to communicate with and why. When you understand your audience and the purpose of your communication, you can begin to determine the best timing—that is, the timing that achieves your objectives, including actively engaging people and carefully accounting for their sensitivities. When planning the timing of any communication consider the best date, how often you will need to communicate and the sequence of events you will need to manage.

> *It isn't always possible to manage the timing of communications, but when feasible here are the most important things you can do:*
>
> ☑ Consider the earliest and latest dates that the information needs to be communicated.
>
> ☑ Reflect on logistics (for example, will it be challenging to gather the group you need to communicate with?).
>
> ☑ Determine whether the communication is a one-off event or an ongoing priority.
>
> ☑ If regular communication is needed, decide how often and the best pattern of timing (weekly, fortnightly or monthly, for example).
>
> ☑ Reflect on whether you need to communicate with certain people ahead of others (for example, because their role warrants it, or out of courtesy or respect).
>
> ☑ Deliver bad news early in the day and week; people don't appreciate this type of news being held back to the end of the day or week (unless that is how circumstances dictate the timing).
>
> ☑ Consider the potential emotional effects and personal consequences of your timing (what can you do to avoid adverse impacts?).

Priority 5: choose the right medium

In the vast majority of cases the ideal medium for communication is face-to-face interaction. While email has its place, communicating in person is the most effective way of achieving clarity and fostering healthy working relationships. Too often people choose to hide behind electronic communications and avoid the conversations they need to have. Conflicts can be created and fuelled by destructive emails that flame emotions and damage trust. Despite these challenges electronic communications can play a valuable role, particularly in allowing us to bridge distance when it isn't possible for everyone to be in the same room.

The most appropriate medium through which to communicate will depend on the content, nature and purpose of the communication. The types of factors you need to consider when deciding which medium will best enable you to achieve your objective include the following:

- Do you need to gather information or provide it?

- Do you want to capture responses in writing or by listening?

- Is it best to explore insights provided straight away or through another step in the process?

- Is more than one communication needed to achieve an objective? For example, could a focus group follow a survey?

- How can you leverage the medium you use to overcome barriers to communication such as geographic location?

Priority 6: select the best setting

The setting you choose for communicating in person can significantly affect the outcome. Some discussions are fine to have in a public place but others are more appropriately convened in the privacy of an office. Some meetings call for a relaxed atmosphere while others need the formality of a meeting room to set the right tone. Think about the physical environment that is most appropriate but also the people who should attend. Consider how the presence of a particular person in the room may influence the way a message is conveyed or received, and whether their presence will aid or hinder honesty and the flow of the conversation. The most important things to determine upfront are whether the forum needs to be private or public, group or individual, and needing either a relaxed or a more formal setting or atmosphere.

If the medium you choose is an email or other written correspondence, should the communication be sent to an individual, a select group or a wider audience? Should certain people be provided with a copy; if so, for what purpose? Including someone on an email distribution list is entirely the same as inviting him or her into a room to join in a conversation. Think about whether, if it was a face-to-face setting, you would choose to invite that person to sit in and observe the meeting. Would that feel appropriate or unnecessary? Also keep in mind that using the 'blind copy' function in email is a risky practice and typically not well received if inadvertently discovered. It is much like inviting someone to hide in the closet and listen in without the knowledge or consent of others present.

Chapter summary: the most important things to do and avoid

Must-do checklist

The most important things you must do for your communication efforts to achieve their objective and have the greatest positive impact include:

✓ understanding your audience and why you are communicating with them

✓ targeting what, how and to whom you communicate to ensure relevance and to add value

✓ demonstrating that you are sincere and authentic

✓ being timely and providing information or feedback when you say you will

(continued)

Chapter summary (cont'd)

✓ facilitating two-way communications to tap into the wisdom and capabilities of your team

✓ being respectful, sensitive and focused on building trust.

Common mistakes to avoid

Among the most common avoidable communication mistakes I observe people managers make are:

✗ *'spinning' a message*—people are perceptive, and more often than not attempts to present information in an unrealistically positive light will be exposed

✗ *telling but not listening*—to be effective, lines of communication must be open in both directions

✗ *being superior*—no matter what your seniority, there is little value in presenting yourself as above or more important than the people you are communicating with

✗ *being overly formal*—be planned and considered but adopt a relaxed and accessible style

✗ *focusing too heavily on planned communications*—the time you spend informally interacting with your team is invaluable.

Chapter 6

Managing performance

Many people fail in life, not for lack of ability or brains or even courage, but simply because they have never organised their energies around a goal.

Elbert Hubbard, writer, publisher, artist, and philosopher

Performance management is so much more than an annual review or document-driven process. Regardless of the systems or forms in place, what really matters is the approach you take every day to getting the best from your team. In this chapter we will explore how to inspire and guide people to reach their full potential by leveraging performance management. We will look at:

- providing clarity about what needs to be achieved and how people are to behave

- the importance of coaching and providing meaningful guidance that helps people to learn and grow

- why accountability and consequences matter as much as they do

- what to do when things aren't going well, such as poor behaviour or substandard outcomes.

Almost every day I observe a significant lost opportunity due to ineffective performance management. A lack of ownership for performance management is evident at all levels of organisations with which I work. Nothing exposes this more than the number of CEOs who regard leaders as performing highly despite their inability to effectively manage the performance of their team. Done well, performance management can have a powerful influence on the success of a business; managed poorly, it can damage morale and waste valuable time and resources.

All too often I hear managers and staff complain that performance management processes add little value while creating additional stress and challenges for everyone involved. It can certainly be argued that some frameworks or systems are flawed, but the real issue typically rests with managers who fail to exploit the opportunity these tools provide. The reality is, it doesn't matter how well designed your performance management systems, processes, forms and policies are. Unless they are effectively applied they add little to no value. Too often managers neglect to set clear expectations, provide useful feedback and hold people accountable—the fundamentals of effective performance management.

What success looks like

Effective performance management requires three essential elements:

- *clarity*—ensuring your team understand what is expected and accepted, important and a priority

- *coaching*—providing feedback, advice and guidance to enable results and ongoing development

- *accountability*—delegating responsibilities, appraising contributions and applying consequences.

Key indicators of a successful approach to performance management include the following:

- People understand what is expected of them and how their performance is measured.

- Managers and staff work together to identify goals and objectives.

- Performance management is a day-to-day process, not just an annual review.

- Staff regularly ask for feedback and guidance from their manager and teammates.

- Team members actively participate in evaluating their own performance.

- Issues are dealt with; managers address poor performance and behaviour.

- People take ownership of their own development and identify growth opportunities.

Clear indicators of an effective performance management process include the following:

- Documented performance and development plans are in place for every member of the team.

- SMART objectives, values and behaviours as well as a development plan are established. (We'll discuss these further on page 130.)

- Performance appraisal meetings are convened on time and considered valuable by all parties.

- All staff complete a self-appraisal and actively participate in performance discussions.

- Accurate and up-to-date records are maintained.

Case study
Coming together

Among the best examples of performance management I have observed is the approach taken by a relatively small and yet diverse manufacturing company I work with. It may seem easy to dismiss the relevance of their example for larger organisations, but at the heart of their approach are ideals and strategies that would serve any business well. With only 80 staff, the complexity of managing this business relates to the breadth of their focus and the geographic dispersion of their team. The organisation is made up of a centralised manufacturing operation, a small finance and administration group and seven teams based in various regional cities across five states. These teams are focused on sales, marketing and customer service targeted to niche market segments.

For many years the organisation struggled to align its efforts and extract value from its collective know-how, approach and resources. When, a number of years ago, they looked at what they did across the team they found a lot of duplication and limited leveraging of their intellectual property and capabilities. Eager to improve performance the business owner hired a new CEO, Mike, who was given licence to dramatically change the business to ensure its success into the future. Many predicted that Mike would restructure the team and centralise the sales and marketing functions; instead he focused on the fundamentals of effective performance management.

Starting with the organisation's vision, Mike spent time listening to the team and sharing his own views about where the company could and should be heading. For the first time in many years the managers from across the business began to come together regularly to discuss shared objectives and strategies for success. Having conversations about their collective performance and how they were progressing towards achieving targets became a frequent and valued activity. Over time this group came to see more opportunities for collaboration and began connecting members of their teams with one another both informally and through the creation of project teams.

Mike is among a small group of CEOs I have observed who genuinely cascade accountability for results down through their organisation. Responsibility for performance starts with him and flows through to the senior members of his team. Mike believes managers hire people, set expectations, coach them and ultimately decide whether or not they remain a member of the team. There is therefore no reasonable excuse, in Mike's view, for a manager to allow performance issues to be left unaddressed or to drag on for too long.

Mike expects every leader to own their role, act with integrity and work hard to influence the success of each member of their team. He holds managers accountable for ensuring their team understand the organisation's goals and how they are expected to contribute. Just as significant is the importance he places on managers having the discipline, courage and skills to manage performance and behaviour.

The responsibility for performance that Mike places on managers, however, does not discount personal accountability. In fact, Mike expects managers to firmly confront anyone who fails to bring a sincere desire to succeed to their role. Mike's managers are compassionate and patient with those who sincerely work hard to improve, but those who show little commitment or engagement are soon asked to leave.

Unsurprisingly, Mike has had a profoundly positive influence on the performance of the team and the business. The challenges created by the breadth of the team's focus and the business's geographic dispersion have shrunk thanks to the strength of the leadership team. People across the business understand the vision and the role they need to play. Also clearly evident is a one-company culture that encourages people to adopt a collaborative and supportive approach to achieving collective success. Compelling indicators of the success of Mike's approach are the 25 per cent revenue growth and the even stronger

38 per cent lift in profits achieved in the first year after he joined the business—neither of which was achieved through staffing cuts. The rate of growth continues to be strong and they enjoy a stable workforce with a 12 per cent annual staff turnover, compared with a previous turnover of between 18 per cent and 24 per cent.

Adopting a strategic approach

Performance management is a significant influencer of organisational culture, staff engagement and ultimately retention. Put simply, the approach adopted can dramatically affect how people feel about working for a business and their manager. Whether or not people choose to stay or strive to be successful is influenced not only by their manager's approach but also by the organisation's collective attitude towards managing performance. An organisation's ability to build a healthy and high-performance culture, earn the trust and respect of its team and optimise performance is influenced by the expectations it sets, how it provides feedback, and the reasonableness of its assessments and decisions relating to reward and recognition.

Strategic performance management begins with the organisation's core objectives, which flow through to every role and person in the team. With a clear vision and strategy, the next step is to identify and articulate the actions to be taken, the outcomes achieved and the behaviours applied by everyone—in other words, what every person on the team needs to do to realise your vision. Strategic performance management demands a balanced focus on the here-and-now contributions people must make but also on the future needs of the business. Focusing on developing capabilities as much as setting expectations and appraising performance is a priority of any forward-looking manager.

Making performance management a priority and investing the energy needed to do it well is critical. A lot of time and energy is expended on creating performance and development plans; it's a waste not to use them. Hours are spent in appraisal meetings; it's a waste not to extract maximum value from the experience. Business performance metrics will ultimately reveal how well your team is performing. Just as important is establishing performance measures that enable you to monitor how well performance management is being applied. Other valuable measures look at elements of an effective performance management process such as those outlined in the 'What success looks like' section of this chapter (see p. 124).

Providing clarity

Ensuring members of your team understand what is expected of them as well as what is considered significant or a priority is the starting point to successfully managing the performance of your team. Without this clarity, the standard of performance achieved may be limited and success uncertain. Providing clarity should start early in the recruitment process and continue during induction and ultimately throughout a team member's employment.

Setting expectations

Performance objectives describe broad categories under which more specific outcomes are defined. They identify essential areas of achievement that enable overall success in a role. Key performance indicators (KPIs) help you to understand how well people are performing in relation to these objectives; they are the measurable factors that enable you to define the success of a particular task or activity and are arrived at in the following way:

- Start by identifying four to six performance objectives — major areas in which performance is essential.

- Next, identify the specific tasks or activities necessary to achieve each objective.

- Finally, establish KPIs, measures of the achievement of performance objectives.

Here is an example in figure 6.1.

Figure 6.1: performance objectives

Performance objective
Effectively manage performance to enable achievement of team goals
Tasks and activities
• Set clear performance expectations and provide ongoing constructive feedback.
• Provide team members with ongoing coaching and development.
• Encourage and reward efforts that achieve strong results and are aligned with our values.
• Proactively celebrate team successes and provide feedback for a job well done.
• Proactively and honestly communicate with team members regarding performance and/or cultural alignment issues.
KPIs
• More than 95 per cent of staff have current performance and development plans in place.
• More than 95 per cent of annual performance appraisals are completed and submitted on time.
• A more than 75 per cent satisfaction rating relating to performance management is reflected in the annual staff survey.
• All (100 per cent) performance concerns identified are resolved through a fair and structured process within a reasonable time frame.

SMART objectives

When establishing performance objectives and associated KPIs, a useful guide is the approach described by the acronym SMART. Designed to guide managers through the process of writing meaningful objectives, the SMART method is widely recognised and applied. It is difficult to know whom to give credit for its creation or the version first recommended; a little research will reveal a profusion of credited sources and variations on the meanings given to each letter. Some of the more commonly used and recognised versions include:

S—specific, stretch, significant

M—measurable, meaningful

A—agreed, achievable, attainable, action-oriented

R—realistic, relevant, reasonable, rewarding, results-oriented

T—time-based, timely, tangible, trackable.

Whichever meanings you choose to apply, using SMART can add value to your thinking and to the quality of the objectives you establish. I have added the acronym PLUS. Setting clear priorities and linking to business goals are key considerations when establishing objectives and setting expectations. Consistent understanding and support further ensure that objectives are achievable.

Described here is the application of the SMART PLUS approach that I most commonly observe.

Specific: the particular result or outcome to be achieved.

☑ Avoid vague or motherhood statements that provide limited insight into what needs to be accomplished.

Measurable: how you will know when the objective has been achieved.

☑ Consider qualitative measures such as observations or feedback (for example, quality of work, client satisfaction).

☑ Include relevant quantitative measures such as number achieved, costs incurred, rate or ratio.

Achievable: challenging but feasible objectives that bring out the best in people.

☑ Avoid impossible objectives that create stress, resistance or resignation to failure.

Relevant: to achievement of a team or organisational goal or strategy.

☑ Make sure people understand why each objective is important or will make a difference.

Time: by which objectives must be achieved.

☑ Determine whether objectives need to be achieved each day or within a specified time period.

☑ Review progress throughout the period.

☑ Establish 'milestone' objectives to achieve along the way towards reaching bigger goals.

Priority: relative to other objectives.

☑ Rank objectives in order of priority to focus efforts.

Link: with how achievement influences broader team objectives.

☑ Enable people to appreciate the consequences of their contribution and performance to the 'bigger picture'.

Understanding: is clear and consistent.

☑ Ensure objectives, priorities and KPIs are uniformly understood by you and your team members.

Support: is available to enable achievement.

☑ Identify and provide the support needed to achieve objectives such as resource capacity, training or guidance.

Adopting a flexible approach

It's common, particularly in more senior roles, for priorities to shift during the year. Adopting a flexible approach will enable you to review objectives regularly throughout the period to ensure they remain relevant and continue to reflect real priorities. How frequently this occurs will vary with the nature and complexity of the role, the rate of change and the particular needs of the business. What matters most is that you and the members of your team treat the performance plan as a living document that reflects the critical drivers of success within the current context.

Involving your team

While it is inevitable that some objectives will be dictated by the nature of the job, others can be agreed on in consultation with your team members. Working with people to identify and agree on what needs to be achieved as well as the standard required can be a powerful way of encouraging engagement with their role. For example, it is reasonable to conclude that a call centre team member will be expected to meet objectives related to call volumes or timeliness. Other objectives, however, such as participating in projects or contributing to the development of team processes, can be targeted not only at team priorities but also according to the individual's capabilities, interests or career ambitions.

Enabling performance

It isn't enough simply to set expectations and forget about them until performance appraisal time. To manage performance well you need to interact with your team every day and provide them with the direction, advice and guidance they need to succeed. To get the best from people, you must challenge their thinking, influence their understanding, encourage them to reflect, and ultimately help them to learn and grow on the job. As we will explore in the sections ahead, a people manager's job is to both manage and coach, to give feedback, make suggestions, be honest about how things are going, and encourage people to keep striving to learn and succeed.

Managing versus coaching

Armed with a clear understanding of what is expected, people are often able to take ownership and get on with the job. Most people, however, regardless of their seniority or experience, need the support of their manager on some level to reach their full potential. Even the most experienced and capable individual will benefit from being managed as well as coached. At times, telling people what to do and even how to approach the task is necessary, but to encourage ownership, facilitate learning and ultimately optimise performance it's crucial to balance managing with coaching.

Knowing when to be the manager and step into the role of directing and when to coach by providing support and guidance is critical to the effectiveness of any people manager. Most people will benefit from an approach that blends the two to an extent that depends on their confidence and capabilities and the complexity of the task at hand. As a general rule you may need to provide greater direction when someone is new in a role, in the company or to working with a particular client or customer. They may also require greater direction when they first take on new job responsibilities and tasks or when the way you go about something has changed. Team members with a moderate to high level of competence can more often, with your support, determine for themselves the approach they will take.

A coach's role is to enable performance by supporting people to explore options and consider potential outcomes. An effective coach asks questions or makes suggestions about what could be considered. They work alongside people, share their own experiences and draw out the best in other people.

To provide coaching support that makes a difference to the performance of your staff, ensure you:

- engage in a two-way process of open dialogue

- provide the guidance needed to support each team member to determine the best approaches

- discuss the progress made as well as the challenges and obstacles they are facing.

Providing effective feedback

Waiting for the annual performance review to let someone know how they are going has limited value, yet this is all too often the approach taken. Unfortunately, by the time that conversation comes around the game is over. Performance objectives will have been achieved or not, and typically there is nothing that can be done except reflect on and document outcomes. The performance review is the formal step in an ongoing process aimed at acknowledging and reflecting on the standard of performance achieved over the period. Appraisal discussions should reflect conversations that have taken place throughout the year.

Providing feedback is an aspect of performance management that commonly needs to improve. Failing to invest time, being unaware of performance standards owing to a lack of monitoring and relying on people to manage themselves are among the causes I have observed. As we will explore later in 'The power of tough love' section of this chapter (see p. 138), other common obstacles to effective feedback relate to the fear and hesitation some people managers feel about initiating the honest conversations needed. It is essential that all managers commit to providing meaningful feedback and developing the skills and willingness they need to do it well.

All of us benefit from acknowledgement and recognition for a job well done as much as from constructive feedback when we need to improve. Unfortunately, however, it is common for managers to consciously observe performance mainly when things go wrong; satisfactory or consistent performance may not always draw attention. Looking for opportunities to catch people doing the right things matters as much as observing what needs to change or improve.

Your feedback can make a significant difference to someone's performance if delivered well. Constructive criticism should be conveyed in ways that help people to understand and avoid a defensive response. Praise and appreciation should be aimed at energising their spirit and encouraging similar behaviours in the future.

The most important things you need to do to provide feedback that makes a tangible difference to performance are described here. Unless specifically stated otherwise, each point relates as much to providing positive as unfavourable feedback.

Priority 1: be specific and descriptive

☑ Describe particular behaviours or outcomes.

☑ Don't make personal judgements or broad generalisations.

☑ Clearly indicate what is unacceptable and needs to change, or what is appreciated and encouraged.

(continued)

Examples:

- 'I am impressed with how well you organised the workshop at such short notice' is considerably more effective than 'I'm pleased with how you're going. Well done', which is largely meaningless.

- 'When you [refer to specific behaviour observed] it's a problem because [refer to specific consequences]. In the future I would like you to [keep doing, start doing, stop doing].'

Priority 2: pick your time and place

☑ Provide feedback as soon as appropriate and practical.

☑ Be sure of the facts before committing to a point of view and providing feedback.

☑ Choose a time that will avoid unnecessary discomfort or disclosure of confidential or sensitive information.

☑ Make sure you are in the right frame of mind to deliver feedback effectively.

☑ Discuss improvement needs or reprimand in a private and confidential setting.

Priority 3: be constructive

☑ Positively influence the self-esteem of the person in the way you deliver feedback.

☑ If performance is below expectations, focus on improvement opportunities rather than just what was unacceptable.

☑ Focus on observations such as 'what' or 'how' something was done.

☑ Avoid statements that may evoke defensiveness such as 'you should have' or 'I can't believe you did that'.

☑ Ask how they think they can address issues.

Priority 4: tailor to the individual

☑ Keep in mind that different approaches work best for different people.

☑ Take into account the individual's character and circumstances when deciding the most effective approach for giving feedback.

Priority 5: be consistent

☑ Build confidence that you apply a consistent approach and standards to all staff.

☑ Provide consistent messages from one day to the next.

Handling feedback pushback

There are many reasons why someone resists feedback and chooses to 'push back'. After questioning and confirming your understanding of the team member's reactions, use these tips to respond:

- If they disagree with your description of the situation:

  - provide more accurate or objective observations

  - include their own experiences, along with other facts they may or may not be aware of.

- If they agree but cite factors that were beyond their control:

  - provide and ask for suggestions of things they can do that are within their control

  - identify ways you can help.

- If they agree but do not see why it is important:

  - describe the significance of the issue including how it affects the team or business or the team member themselves.

- If they agree but say their intention was different:

  - acknowledge their intentions and reinforce the consequences of their approach

  - encourage better awareness and greater accountability.

The power of tough love

The single most important aspect of a people manager's approach to managing performance is tough love—that is, being completely honest while delivering feedback with compassion and sensitivity. An empowering and respectful process, tough love demands that you deliver fair and necessary feedback with conviction and kindness. While telling the truth can be an opportunity to help people understand and take ownership of their performance, if not delivered well it won't work. Brutal honesty on its own can be destructive or inspire defensiveness. Avoiding the truth, on the other hand, can be equally damaging as it holds people back from reaching their potential and ultimately succeeding.

Time and time again I observe managers avoiding the difficult conversations they need to have. Some worry about how the person will react, while others shrink from the discomfort they themselves will feel. Some managers are driven by kindness and simply don't want to make the team member feel bad. Others justify avoiding the issue to themselves by arguing that criticism risks further diminishing the person's confidence and performance.

While these are valid challenges, people managers have a responsibility to overcome such barriers and provide constructive feedback. It is critical that you tell people the truth and own your responsibility for ensuring that every member of your team knows what they are capable of as well as how they need to improve. It is a matter of integrity that you do the job you signed up for and get past your own fears and comfort level to conduct the difficult conversations that can make such a crucial difference to success.

Accountability

Unless there are consequences—reward and recognition when things go well; remedial action when they don't—it is unlikely your team will take performance management seriously. Setting expectations people know you won't follow through on adds little value; if your staff don't believe it matters to you, they won't believe it matters to them.

Shared ownership and self-assessment

While it is true that every leader has an opportunity and obligation to drive performance management, personal ownership matters just as much. For the best possible results, accountability for the performance of each individual must be shared between that person and their manager. Every manager is accountable for providing clarity, coaching and a healthy workplace environment. Every team member is accountable for their own capabilities, spirit and performance.

Shared ownership can be encouraged by expecting your staff to play an equally active role in the performance management process throughout the year. Every member of the team should be expected to evaluate their own performance and contribute to identifying their development needs. Using self-assessment in the appraisal process typically promotes a less authoritarian culture and provides for a more satisfying and constructive performance discussion. At the end of a review cycle ask your staff to complete a self-appraisal by rating their performance against agreed KPIs, including behavioural indicators. Self-assessment results can then be compared against your own views and observations and discussed during the review meeting.

To encourage participation throughout the process, ask every member of your team to:

- regularly review their performance and development plan to ensure its ongoing relevance

- proactively monitor their own progress towards achieving key objectives and seeking input or guidance as required to enable success

- keep a diary of their accomplishments, including results achieved throughout the year

- be prepared to discuss their achievements against objectives, to emphasise results and how those results were achieved

- be prepared to discuss their specific development objectives for the next review period

- in preparation for appraisal discussions, gather together materials that reflect their performance and achievements, including feedback from midterm reviews, colleagues or customers.

Evaluating performance

Assessment or rating scales included in many performance management frameworks are designed to distinguish between levels of performance to reflect standards of achievement against key objectives. Whether or not the process you work with requires you to provide a performance rating, it remains necessary that you tell people specifically the standard to which they have achieved each objective. Most people are also eager to hear how their overall performance is perceived.

When measuring or rating performance it is critical to remain objective and to view performance in light of measurable objectives and observable behaviours. While most people managers work through performance appraisals with sincere intentions, there is some risk of ratings being influenced, consciously or otherwise, by favouritism, prejudice, unfounded perceptions or even workplace relationships.

Here are the most important things you must do to ensure performance ratings are fair and consistent:

☑ Evaluate based on specific objectives rather than a single overall impression of good or bad performance.

☑ Consider work completed throughout the period, not just shortly before the performance review.

☑ Look for evidence and consider the facts rather than unfounded assumptions or perceptions.

☑ Resist tendencies to rate as a group, giving everyone either a low, average or high rating.

☑ Apply objective and consistent criteria to determine the standard of performance achieved.

☑ Avoid being influenced by employee styles or backgrounds similar to or different from your own.

Performance review meetings

Daily interactions and conversations underpin a successful approach, but taking the time to deliberately reflect and discuss performance is crucial. More structured discussions should occur at least monthly. This does not necessarily imply a heavy time commitment or onerous workload. These discussions can form part of the regular one-on-one meetings you should be having with your staff. Take the time to pull out their performance and development plan, run through the key deliverables that fall due in the period ahead and reflect on those that have already occurred. Elicit their input on how things are going and explore ways in which obstacles or challenges can be overcome.

An annual or six-monthly performance review is commonly the formal step in the appraisal process. Depending on the approach taken, performance reviews can have a significant positive or negative impact. Their success will depend on the work you have done throughout the year to ensure clarity of expectations and to communicate frequently and effectively.

Preparation

The preparation you and each team member do leading up to a performance review meeting will greatly influence the success and value of the exercise.

Here are the most important things you must do to prepare for a performance review or appraisal meeting:

☑ Secure a quiet and confidential venue away from the immediate work space and interruptions.

☑ Review set objectives and ask your team member to do the same.

☑ Consider your assessment of each objective, expected behaviour and commitment to learning.

☑ Write down examples that demonstrate the way in which objectives were achieved or behaviours reflected.

☑ Review the performance rating scale to determine the most appropriate rating. Be careful of leniency, strictness or choosing the easy option by giving everyone the same rating.

Facilitation

The way you choose to facilitate performance review meetings can profoundly influence the way people feel about and respond to the outcome of their appraisal. Optimal value can be achieved only if the members of your team believe their contribution has been reviewed in a fair and considered way.

Here are the most important things you must do to facilitate an effective performance review meeting:

- ☑ Provide both overall and specific feedback about key objectives.

- ☑ Ensure there are no surprises; don't raise issues for the first time in a review.

- ☑ Avoid raising old issues (those that have been addressed in previous appraisal periods and are no longer a concern).

- ☑ Ask people to take you through their self-appraisal of each objective and behaviour.

- ☑ Share your appraisal and discuss areas of strong agreement or disagreement.

- ☑ Talk through differences to ensure they understand the reasons for your assessment.

- ☑ Listen to the individual's perspective and be open to having your perceptions shifted (never compromise the rating you truly believe is warranted, however).

- ☑ Confirm common understandings of what has been agreed and final ratings.

If your team member strongly disagrees with your appraisal, it is often necessary to schedule a follow-up meeting. Assure them you will reflect further on their feedback and request that they do the same with the feedback you have provided them. There is little point in being locked in disagreement; reconvening a day or two later may give your team member time to process and come to terms with your assessment. Of course it will also give you the opportunity to consider any aspects of their appraisal that should reasonably change in light of their self-assessment.

Ultimately you are responsible for determining a final appraisal that accurately reflects their performance. If no agreement can be reached after fair and reasonable discussion, make your decision and ask the employee to sign off their appraisal document to indicate your discussions have taken place. They do not need to acknowledge agreement with your appraisal, only that they have formally met with their manager and discussed their performance as it relates to the appraisal period.

Managing poor performance

When informal coaching and feedback haven't worked to improve performance, the next step is to formalise the process. Taking a more planned and structured approach can help focus your efforts and provide the individual with the understanding, guidance and support they need. The goal of performance counselling should always be to help people improve and to become a more successful member of your team. At some point, however, most managers will be faced with the decision to end a team member's employment. Knowing you have done everything in your power to help the person to succeed is the best way to be at peace with the integrity of these decisions.

Priority 1: identify the problem

Adopting a hands-on approach to people management will best position you to observe and identify performance challenges as they arise. Early detection allows you to take steps to resolve the issue before seriously detrimental impacts occur. While being optimistic is essential, so too is recognising the truth for what it is. Denying evidence or signals of poor performance benefits no-one. If your gut instinct or early observations suggest someone is struggling in their role, take appropriate action before the issue becomes more complex and difficult to resolve.

Priority 2: accurately diagnose the problem

The first step towards improving poor performance is understanding and articulating the difference between what is happening and what should be happening. Often I work with leaders who struggle to identify the specific issue they are dealing with, let alone put strategies in place to enable improvement.

To be well prepared for a discussion with your team member, ensure you:

- understand the gap between current and required performance
- appreciate the seriousness of the problem, including its ramifications
- recognise potential contributing factors.

Following are a series of questions designed to guide you in exploring contributing factors and consequences of performance problems.

What is the performance discrepancy?

- What does success look like and how does it differ from the current standard of performance? Consider:
  - the specific behaviour being performed or not being performed
  - the outcome being achieved or not being achieved.

How important is it?

- What would happen if the issue were left unaddressed? To what extent will it affect achievement of key priorities?

Does the person know what is expected?

- Are key objectives and expected behaviours clearly defined and articulated?
- Is a lack of clarity about priorities contributing to the issue?
- Are your standards clear? (Does the person understand what constitutes poor, average or good performance?)

Are your expectations reasonable?

- Given your team member's capabilities, the resources available and the environment in which they are working, is it likely they will be able to deliver?

- Have you provided the training necessary to equip them with the knowledge or skills they need?

- Are there competing priorities that make achievement unreasonably challenging?

Is it a skill or knowledge deficiency?

- Are their skills adequate for the level of performance required?

  − Do they need to develop new skills?

  − Do they need to know how to apply their capabilities more effectively?

- Could they do it if their job depended on it? If yes, is the issue motivation and engagement?

- Could they do it in the past? Have they lost interest? Are they feeling demotivated or bored?

- Is the skill used often? Is it possible that they have forgotten how to do it?

Are there obstacles to performance?

- Are external factors preventing them from performing well? For example, are there:

  − conflicting demands on their time?

  − restrictive policies that prevent the job from being done well?

  − physical distractions that interfere with performance?

- Are personal issues interfering with their ability to perform?

Are there consequences that discourage performance?

- Is it punishing to perform as desired?

  - Are you inadvertently discouraging good performance by creating disadvantages for those who succeed (for example, assigning heavier workloads and greater responsibility to more productive team members with no reward or recognition)?

Priority 3: raise the issue with your team member

The next step is to discuss the performance issue with your team member. In some cases an accurate diagnosis of the problem will require you to first discuss the issue with the person. In others you will be able to form an accurate view of the underlying issues before raising them with the person. Your primary goal is to ensure they clearly understand what the problem is, why it's a problem, how it influences the workplace or the team's success, and what the potential consequences are.

Here are some of the most important things you need to do to optimise the positive impact of raising the issue with your team member:

☑ Consider the meeting environment. You should not be visible to others and should be free of any form of interruption.

☑ Introduce the issue or topic and provide feedback in a straightforward yet sensitive manner.

  ☑ Speak clearly and do not rush.

  ☑ Keep your tone serious but compassionate.

(continued)

- ☑ Briefly and succinctly state the purpose of the meeting.

- ☑ Avoid idle chatter about irrelevant topics—get straight to the point.

- ☑ Avoid having or projecting an 'attitude', such as:

  - ☑ 'I shouldn't have to tell you . . .' Perhaps, but you do have to tell them, so move on.

  - ☑ 'You should know better . . .' Maybe they are not aware or don't understand the consequences of their actions.

  - ☑ 'This isn't my job . . .' Actually it is; managing performance is every people manager's job.

  - ☑ 'I have no idea what your problem is . . .' Never be dismissive; it helps no-one.

- ☑ Provide assurance of your commitment to supporting them.

  - ☑ If reprimanding a team member for misconduct, it may be more appropriate to express a desire to see them succeed and take responsibility for ensuring the issue doesn't persist or recur.

  - ☑ Acknowledge the seriousness of the matter, but express your hope and optimism for a positive outcome.

Priority 4: agree on a performance improvement plan

All too often I observe managers and staff going through the motions of a performance counselling process and becoming locked in disagreement. Unless the team member accepts that they need to improve and takes ownership for making it happen, they are unlikely to succeed. Put simply, if they are unwilling or believe they don't need to do the work it takes to improve, then they won't. While at times challenging, it's necessary to work with people to develop and agree on performance improvement plans. If they resist these plans unreasonably, point out that their attitude is likely to obstruct efforts to resolve the issues successfully.

Here are some of the most important things you must do when developing a performance improvement plan:

☑ Establish clear improvement objectives including:

    ☑ minimum standards of improvement expected immediately and in the near term

    ☑ ultimate standards of performance required, including behaviours that must be consistently demonstrated and outcomes that must be consistently achieved

    ☑ how progress will be monitored and success measured.

☑ Consider and explore training and other development options where relevant.

☑ Set realistic time frames that provide reasonable opportunity to meet improvement expectations.

☑ Schedule the next meeting within two weeks to discuss progress. In cases of gross underperformance more frequent meetings may be needed, especially early in the process.

Priority 5: monitor and influence improvement progress

Throughout the performance counselling process it is essential that you maintain a hands-on approach, with regular interactions and discussions between you and your team member. Helping someone to overcome performance challenges takes an equal level of commitment from both parties.

Success in many ways depends on what the person in question believes is possible. It's essential to focus not only on what is going wrong but also on reasons for hope and a belief that they can improve. Take time to highlight what is working and any indicators you see of their potential to bounce back. Reflect on past success and well-developed capabilities they have to draw on.

Avoid being pedantic. Even high performers make mistakes. People shouldn't feel pressure to be perfect and some lapses should be reasonably discounted. While not always the best place to start, it can also help to encourage people to recognise that failing isn't the end of the world. Everyone has gifts that, when applied to their work, can help them achieve amazing success. There are many paths to a happy and successful work life — your team member just needs to find the right one for them.

Here are the most important things you can do to influence improvement progress:

☑ Continue to monitor performance and provide timely feedback and guidance.

☑ Balance discussions between offering constructive feedback and providing positive reinforcement.

☑ Nurture their spirit to build hope and confidence. Help them to maintain the positive energy they need to keep striving.

Priority 6: reach quality outcomes

Once competence is demonstrated consistently over a reasonable period of time, formalised performance counselling can be concluded. If the required improvements have not been achieved, however, it will ultimately become necessary to end the person's employment in their role. At this point, some organisations make the mistake of either tolerating underperformance or transferring the problem to another team or area of the business. Offering a low-performing team member a different role is a good idea only if they are qualified and as likely as another strong candidate to succeed.

To reach outcomes that are in the best interests of the business and the team member concerned, make sure you:

- adopt an approach based on respect, fairness and compassion

- do the person and your business a favour: if the best role for them is outside of your business, then let them go.

- consider getting legal advice to ensure your decisions are lawful.

Priority 7: document the process

To support your ability to manage and demonstrate a fair process, it's essential that you document all performance- or behaviour-related conversations.

Here are some of the most important things to do and consider when documenting the process:

☑ Document reasons for discussions, key points raised and action plans agreed on.

☑ Provide the team member with a summary of the discussion and agreed outcomes. Keep a copy for your records.

☑ To ensure accuracy, complete your notes within 24 hours of each meeting.

(continued)

- ☑ Ask the team member to sign the file note to confirm their understanding of the information and agreement that it accurately reflects the discussion that took place.
  - ☑ If they don't want to sign, make a note of this on the document.
  - ☑ Allow them to add their own comments to the file note if they wish; you do not need to agree with them.
- ☑ Documentation is essential if your actions or decisions are challenged through relevant tribunals or courts.
  - ☑ File and meeting notes should be drafted and kept, bearing in mind that they could be needed in a legal proceeding.
  - ☑ Ensure the accuracy of your note taking and remain factual at all times; avoid personal opinions or bias.

Priority 8: monitor your approach

Valuable questions to ask yourself to assess the integrity and effectiveness of your approach throughout the performance coaching (or improvement) process include the following:

- Are you communicating honestly and with compassion?
- Is your sincere intention to help the team member to be successful in their role?
- Does it feel right? If a process or decision doesn't feel right, it probably isn't!
- Have you set and maintained realistic time frames?
- Are you providing adequate support to facilitate learning?
- Have you considered and addressed all contributing factors?

Dealing with poor behaviour

The performance improvement process already described applies regardless of whether the issue you are dealing with relates to capability or behaviour. However, dealing with inappropriate conduct can create particular challenges and present unique priorities. Among the more common examples of poor behaviours I observe in workplaces are:

- gossiping about and unfairly or harshly criticising colleagues

- rude, aggressive or disrespectful conduct

- constant complaining due to a pessimistic outlook

- withdrawal, sulking or other forms of passive aggressive behaviour

- bad manners and inability to be polite and courteous.

As common as these issues are, challenging individuals about unacceptable behaviour can be confronting and daunting for many managers, yet it is their job to deal with them. The team member responsible should be told the truth about how they are affecting others, and the rest of the team need you to step in and change the situation. The first step you need to take is making the commitment to address the issue.

Here are the most important things you need to do and consider when dealing with behavioural issues:

☑ Remember, the behaviours you accept and endorse through your actions or inaction drive the culture you create.

☑ How people behave matters as much as what they achieve, so hold even your highest achieving team member accountable for behaving appropriately.

(continued)

☑ Poor behaviour or misconduct is not aligned with the values of the business or reasonable expectations of professional conduct.

☑ Never accept claims of naivety as an excuse; acknowledge an absence of ill will but reinforce the individual's responsibility for their own conduct.

☑ Maintain composure. Some behaviours can be annoying or frustrating; if you feel upset take time to regain composure before addressing the issue.

☑ Be sensitive. The individual may be unaware that their behaviour is inappropriate; they could find the feedback confronting and even embarrassing.

☑ Be clear. Explain the consequences of their behaviour, and ensure they understand.

☑ Look past the behaviour to the underlying emotions, where you will often find the real cause and therefore the solution to the problem.

☑ Show compassion. Poor behaviour often reflects a drained spirit.

    ☑ You can be firm and uncompromising while kind; in other words, use tough love.

    ☑ Look for ways to help people be happier and their behaviours may well improve.

    ☑ They may be happier if they leave your organisation.

☑ In cases of serious misconduct, if there is not reasonable cause for lawful instant dismissal then take a firm stance: specify non-negotiable expectations of improvement and the consequences of failing to comply.

☑ Observe discreetly and follow up swiftly when needed.

Chapter summary: the most important things to do and avoid

For performance management to have any real impact on achieving your vision and objectives, every member of the team has a role to play. Shared accountability is crucial, with success resting with managers and staff alike. Unless driven from the top, however, performance management is unlikely to be effective.

Must-do checklist

The non-negotiable roles and responsibilities that drive the success of performance management in any business are described here.

Business owners, CEOs and senior managers must:

✓ make performance management matter; follow through and hold people accountable

✓ demonstrate commitment and lead by example

✓ communicate vision, goals, priorities and strategies that can be cascaded down through the organisation

✓ invest in the development of leaders and their ability to manage performance well.

Every people manager must:

✓ encourage and inspire people to strive for success

✓ communicate clear performance standards and expectations, linking them to the big picture

✓ manage performance fairly, consistently and accurately

✓ be courageous—take action, initiate the difficult conversations and apply consequences

✓ be well informed of the individual's progress through observation and obtaining feedback

(continued)

Chapter summary (cont'd)

✓ provide and openly discuss feedback about how people are going and how they can improve

✓ listen to the staff member's views and openly discuss them

✓ be open to both positive and negative feedback from the staff member

✓ be sensitive and empathetic to the challenges people face

✓ recognise and reward a job well done, both informally and formally

✓ proactively develop the capabilities of individuals and the team

✓ appropriately maintain confidentiality.

Common mistakes to avoid

The biggest mistakes I observe people managers make that limit their ability to effectively leverage performance management include:

✗ failing to dedicate the time and energy needed to manage a value-adding process

✗ failing to establish SMART objectives

✗ limiting set objectives to those that can be quantitatively measured

✗ focusing only on the year-end appraisal rather than coaching throughout the year

✗ facilitating a one-sided process, with limited ownership or contribution from team members

✗ lacking compassion or sensitivity when addressing issues

✗ failing to provide constructive feedback and avoiding difficult conversations.

Chapter 7

Learning and development

*The only thing worse than training employees and losing them,
is not training them and keeping them.*

Zig Ziglar, best-selling author and motivational speaker

Investing time and energy on learning and development is one of those 'I know I should, but…' topics for many of the leaders I work with. Most understand how necessary it is to build on their team's capabilities but few give learning and development the focus it deserves. As we explored in earlier chapters, capabilities are the things people know, the skills they have, and their ability to apply their knowledge and skills effectively in particular circumstances. In this chapter we will explore what managers must do to develop the capabilities of the people already on their team. We will look at:

- the importance of 'growing your own' and investing in learning

- developing a culture that supports learning objectives

- how to create a targeted development plan for each member of your team

- getting value from facilitated learning solutions such as training, coaching and mentoring

- why experience is the greatest teacher and self-reflection its strongest ally.

Beyond influencing success, providing people with the chance to learn and grow is crucial to keeping them with your business. Training and the opportunity to learn new things on the job are among the most commonly stated reasons people give for choosing to join, stay or leave an organisation. To retain their talent, leaders must play an active, hands-on role in supporting members of their team to develop their capabilities and progress in their careers.

All leaders should be held accountable for developing their teams proactively, but just as necessary is expecting each person to take ownership of their own development. Leaders should expect and inspire people to strive to keep growing throughout their employment, and indeed their careers, recognising the truth that we can always learn more. Even those staff not looking to take another step up the ladder of career progression can continue to learn and endeavour to excel in their job.

What success looks like

The ultimate indicator of the effectiveness of your learning and development efforts is your ability to access talent from within your business when you need to. Having the capabilities needed to achieve your strategic objectives at every step is the primary objective of developing your team. A strong learning culture in which people are not only encouraged to keep learning but actively pursue development opportunities is a powerful indicator of success.

Managers who effectively manage learning and development do the following:

- balance their focus on development initiatives that address short-term needs with those focused on longer term objectives
- take a hands-on approach to coaching their team

- encourage members of their team to have a clear view of what they want to create in their career

- guide their staff to identify the capabilities they need to improve and grow further

- ensure every member of their team has in place a documented learning and development plan.

Key indicators of a team member's commitment to their own learning and development include:

- a healthy ego reflected in self-belief balanced with a strong desire to learn

- honest personal reflection with the courage to be vulnerable and the willingness to change

- motivation to look for opportunities to learn through experience

- seeking out mentors able to guide the way

- asking for help and guidance when needed to overcome challenges in their role.

Case study
Learning journey

For many years I worked for The Vanguard Group, one of the world's largest investment management companies. A recognised leader in the industry, Vanguard enjoys a long and proud history of success. Central to Vanguard's business strategy has always been a focus on and commitment to leveraging the full potential of their people. In the minds of the senior Vanguard leaders I worked with, supporting their staff to learn and grow was recognised as a key competitive advantage for which all people managers were held responsible.

During my time with Vanguard I witnessed countless examples of staff being given the opportunity to take on new or more senior positions. When CEO and founder John Bogle retired, the appointment of his successor, Jack Brennan, came from within the business. When Jack Brennan left the top post, the next appointed CEO was yet another Vanguard veteran, Bill McNabb. Far from being limited to the highest office in the company, internal appointments and promotions were common at Vanguard and considered a critical strategy. Not only were Vanguard leaders committed to providing career advancement opportunities, but they were equally committed to supporting their staff to develop the capabilities needed to take those steps. Growing future leaders was recognised as being particularly important.

Underpinning the success of Vanguard's approach to talent management was a culture of continuous improvement and learning. Equally influential was the belief that significant competitive advantage is created through building a talented and engaged workforce. Providing career paths that delivered opportunities for people to learn and grow with the business was central to Vanguard's people management strategies and their success.

In November 2012 Drexel University's LeBow College of Business published online an interview with Vanguard Chairman and CEO Bill McNabb. In a revealing account of Vanguard's talent management strategies Bill discusses the importance of focusing on talent development, commitment to experiential learning and investment in formal training. Listening to Bill, it's clearly evident that Vanguard's commitment to learning and development remains as strong as when I worked with them close to a decade ago.

In the interview Bill talks about the competitive advantage of Vanguard's approach to development and points to their low staff turnover as a key benefit. 'If you look at our turnover rates versus most…in the financial services world I think the average turnover is about 25 per cent; we're running at about 6 per cent.' Bill goes on to suggest that staff retention is critical to success and providing development opportunities is central to their ability to keep their best talent. 'People are coming to us for a career not just a job and I think it's a huge advantage.'

Perhaps one of the most powerful aspects of Vanguard's approach is their focus on developing capabilities needed by the business, not just a particular job or department. Vanguard's 'one company' culture encourages people to focus on the needs of the business as a whole. This attitude is reflected in Bill's comments. 'We're big believers in experiential learning so we try to move people around quite a bit. It's not uncommon for someone to serve in our retirement business and then move over to our retail business and then maybe move over to an internal staff position. That experiential growth helps people reinvent themselves almost organically if you will.'

On this point, Bill continues, 'If you were to look at the career paths of any of our more senior folks they don't make sense. People have taken on assignments, done different things and it doesn't look like an orderly progression because it usually is not. We find that's actually very beneficial. We want people who have the flexibility and frankly the capability to move across a lot of different domains'.

Vanguard's commitment to learning and development creates a clear and distinct competitive advantage, the benefits of which are likely to be enjoyed well into the future. Regardless of the size or resources available to an organisation, a great deal can be learned from the priority Vanguard managers place on deliberately and purposefully growing the capabilities of their team.

Adopting a strategic approach

Adopting a strategic approach to learning and development means first identifying the core objectives of your organisation, the team or a role. Then you need to understand the context within which these objectives must be achieved, including any obstacles, challenges or complexities the team or person is likely to encounter. Once you understand what needs to be achieved and within what context, you can identify the core competencies required. You need to consider not only the technical competencies, but also the broader organisational, emotional, cognitive and interpersonal capabilities that will underpin success.

Often, though, there is a lack of clarity about the competencies we expect people to demonstrate, including at what standard, in which circumstances and for what reasons. Every supervisor, up through the senior leadership team, needs to understand intimately the 'must-have' (as opposed to 'nice-to-have') knowledge, skills and experience required by each role in their team. With this awareness, managers can not only set clear expectations, but also make effective decisions about learning and development priorities. It is every people manager's job to understand which skills are mission critical and which, while valuable, are less likely to make a significant difference to success.

Grow your own talent

As we touched on in chapter 4, among the most effective ways to develop the capabilities of your business is to adopt a 'grow-your-own' strategy. This means focusing on developing your existing team's leadership and specialist technical competencies in preference to hiring them in from outside the organisation. Developing an effective strategy starts by looking at your organisation's strategic plan, identifying capabilities that will enable future success and competitiveness, and developing learning solutions to deliberately foster these competencies.

A grow-your-own strategy allows you to access key capabilities when needed, such as appointing new leaders from within as opportunities arise. Appointing managers and senior leaders from among your own troops is a powerful way to build a consistent, culturally aligned approach from all leaders. People who have 'grown up' in the business and been promoted into management roles because they are both capable and cultural ambassadors are those most likely to enable success. Certain unique skill sets or industry knowledge can also often be best developed internally, reducing the risks inherent in being strongly dependent upon the external market.

Career development and progression will influence any business's ability to retain engaged and high-performing staff. By adopting a grow-your-own strategy you send a strong signal to your people that you are interested in and committed to their professional development and advancement. In addition to keeping talented people over the longer term, a grow-your-own strategy enables maximum flexibility: with well-trained talent waiting in the wings, an organisation is more strongly placed to respond to shifting conditions and demands.

Invest in learning and development

Only with a strategic, planned, ongoing approach to learning and development will you successfully build the capabilities of your team in a way that enables the organisation to reach the heights of its potential. A critical priority for any organisation is to invest in the growth of leadership capabilities, which in turn enables leaders to guide the growth and development of their team. Continuous learning and development must be valued by every person in the organisation. Unless there is real support for a grow-your-own approach it will be a difficult objective to achieve in practice.

Create a learning culture

A strong culture of learning promotes the growth of the business's capabilities, even when being too busy could easily become an excuse. People with a thirst to learn are more likely to make learning a priority and create space for it in their lives. Powerful learning cultures also break down hierarchical and other prejudicial boundaries to sharing wisdom throughout the organisation. Any obstacles to learning are removed. People are encouraged to actively support one another to grow; without exception, they are expected to remain open-minded to what they don't know and ways in which they need to improve.

A culture of continuous learning is a powerful enabler of building team capabilities. As with making a grow-your-own strategy work, leaders need to lead by example and place a high value on ongoing learning opportunities. Company policies and programs should actively encourage people to continue their studies; leaders should demonstrate commitment by dedicating time and resources to training; and staff should be expected to fulfil their end of the bargain by being open to, and actively pursuing, learning. Not only must leaders implement learning solutions; they must operate with an open mind—and, where appropriate, wallet—towards allowing people to pursue reasonable learning goals that relate to their work or the interests of the business.

Begin with induction

Focus and commitment to the learning and development of each team member should begin with a well-considered and -planned induction program. The program should be aimed at helping your new team members to quickly integrate into the organisation and get up to speed with their role. The longer you take to give people the information, guidance and resources they need to succeed, the longer it will take for them to begin to add value and achieve the objectives of their role. A crucial component of any induction process is communication of your performance management process, including the approach taken to ongoing professional development. New team members should have clearly defined performance objectives, but they should also have a development plan.

Creating a development plan

Successful teams have people with the knowledge, skills and behaviours needed to fulfil their mandate and achieve their goals. Assessing the extent to which a team's existing capabilities are adequate to meet current and future business needs is an ongoing priority. A formalised annual review is a good starting point to ensuring you regularly look for capability gaps and put plans in place to bridge them. Development plans should be created for both the organisation as a whole and each member of the team.

When creating development plans for individuals on your team, remember there is no one-size-fits-all approach that will work for all people in all circumstances. In each case identify the specific capability gaps that need to be bridged and the best way this can be achieved. A plan that is well thought out and designed can help your staff grow in their current roles and develop capabilities that will allow them to fulfil their career aspirations over time.

Typically the best development plans involve a blend of strategies that collectively influence individual growth. These strategies include activities that can be categorised as facilitated, experiential and self-learning. Some will play a more important role than others, but more often than not the development plan needed will incorporate an element of each. Later in this chapter we will explore each of these learning strategies and how they can best be applied to ensure a return on investment in time and money.

For any development plan to add value, accountability must be shared between the manager and the team member. Both should be expected to create carefully considered plans that lay out specific capabilities and any change of competence targeted. The team member should be encouraged and expected to play an active role in identifying the learning solutions that will be implemented. Unless the individual is fully engaged and wants to learn, they are unlikely to get there. Allowing them to play an active role in determining the approach taken helps to enable ultimate success of the initiative.

Priority 1: development objectives and target capabilities

In most cases it will be appropriate to focus on two or three development objectives (that is, the broad areas of competence that need to be learned or improved). For each development objective it is necessary also to identify the specific knowledge and skills required.

For example, it's not enough to say that improving communication is a priority; a well-developed plan will articulate specifically what about communication needs to change. Following are the types of contextual questions to explore when creating a targeted development plan for this competency:

- Does the person need to be able to engage articulately in pure information exchange, or does she need to be able to persuade someone to accept a different point of view?

- If persuasion and influence matter in communication, how tough a challenge will it be to apply these capabilities?

- Will she have a difficult audience—and if so, in what ways?

- Will she be constantly faced with fundamentally stubborn people, or will she be expected to influence political agendas?

- How confidential and sensitive is the information (or circumstances) under which she will operate?

- To what degrees will her communications require diplomacy or compassionate expression?

- Will she be expected to educate or just tell?

- Will she usually be asking or sharing when she communicates with others?

Priority 2: development solutions

Focusing on the end game—that is, the change we want to create—helps us to identify the development solutions most likely to work. In many instances, it will be necessary to leverage more than one initiative or solution to support a team member to achieve a development objective or grow in a particular competency area. For example, in many cases a combination of formalised training and manager coaching would be expected.

Be creative and think broadly when development planning. For example, training programs can play a valuable role but may not always be the best solution. The types of development solutions you should consider incorporating into a plan include:

- on-the-job activities or project participation

- training courses and workshops

- coaching or mentoring

- training in another job, either within the same team or in another department

- attendance at seminars and conferences.

Decisions about which development solution to leverage should be based in part on how each has participants engage with the process of learning. For instance, does the learning initiative have them predominantly listening, with limited mental or verbal processing, or are they actively putting concepts they have learned into practice in real or realistic scenarios? Both learning approaches are appropriate at times, but for any given learning program it's essential to understand which approach will add the greatest value.

Theory can be a relevant starting point particularly when building awareness, but real shifts of competence are possible only when people have the opportunity to practise the skill in similar or simulated circumstances. Not only should the learning programs themselves encourage application, but the manager should also look for opportunities to enable people to apply what they have learned on the job. There is little point in someone learning something at a workshop but then not having the opportunity to put it into practice. The sooner someone is able to apply what they have learned the more likely it is that the learning will be cemented.

It is imperative that you review progress continually throughout the life of the development plan to ensure solutions are being implemented and intended learning objectives are being achieved.

Priority 3: involvement of others

Once you have identified appropriate development solutions, the next step is to find the best facilitators. In some instances it will make sense to first look internally for potential candidates. Don't underestimate the capabilities you already have on your team. While your current staff may not always be the most experienced teachers, there are likely to be circumstances when they can make a positive difference in the development of their colleagues. Also keep in mind that teaching can itself be a great teacher, and coaching their peers can be a valuable experience for both parties.

If no-one internally is able to facilitate what you need, then the next best approach is tapping into your networks for referrals. You may in some instances already know providers who have delivered or have a strong reputation. If not, ask other people in your business community who they recommend and why. In the 'Facilitated learning' section of this chapter we will explore the essential selection criteria for a quality learning program provider.

Priority 4: establishing target dates

Among the most common challenges in achieving learning objectives is implementing plans with discipline. Many managers struggle to create the plans in the first place, and often they are then forgotten until the next review. This is far from a management challenge alone; too few people take personal accountability for making sure they get the training or development opportunities they need to learn and grow. Learning outcomes are hardly thought about during the year and are therefore rarely realised by the end of it.

One way to help overcome these challenges is to commit to deadlines or target delivery dates. Simply to promise 'sometime this year' is typically not enough to keep people focused on making it happen. Wherever possible, elect a date by which a learning program will be commenced and completed. If it is not possible to nominate completion dates, establish milestone dates at which time you will review progress. The same principle should be applied to learning programs that are ongoing throughout the year, such as coaching. In these cases it is equally crucial to set review or progress dates to occur at periodic intervals. Consider the outline of a development plan shown in figure 7.1.

Figure 7.1: development plan outline

Development objective	A well-developed ability to administer payroll processes
Target behaviour or capability	Ability to autonomously and accurately: • add new staff to the payroll system • make changes to employee payroll records • process time-keeping data
Involvement of others	• payroll manager • XYZ Company
Development solutions	
• Attend 'Foundations of Payroll Processing' training course provided by XYZ Company	To be completed by July
• On-the-job training: assist the payroll manager with fortnightly payroll processing	Ongoing

Learning methods

There are many different ways people learn and develop their capabilities. In this section we will look more closely at those most commonly applied, including facilitated programs such as training and coaching, learning through experience, and the benefits of self-guided development opportunities such as reading and reflection.

Facilitated learning

Facilitated learning solutions such as coaching, training courses and workshops can aid development significantly if the right options are chosen for the right reasons. For example, there is little value in an effective delegation course when the real development need is to improve communication. Similarly, a training course will have limited positive effect if hands-on experience in putting theory into practice is needed. In that case coaching may be a more effective learning solution. Only when facilitated programs are targeted to specific circumstances and learning needs can they have a positive influence on development that extends beyond improving general knowledge or awareness.

All too often I observe poor choices made about development programs for leaders and staff. The quick-fix or generic solutions that are often implemented have very little impact on improving capabilities. Some organisations rush into engaging the services of learning program providers without giving appropriate consideration to their track record, credentials or approach. Every person and organisation you engage to facilitate a workshop, deliver a training program, or coach a group or individual can affect your team positively or negatively and should therefore be carefully selected.

Strong facilitators skilled at developing trusted adviser relationships can dramatically shift perceptions and encourage behaviours in those they work with, so it's crucial that the messages they deliver are aligned with the values and priorities of your business. It's just as crucial that they deliver targeted content relevant to achieving the specific learning objective. Beware of those providers who promise targeted solutions and yet deliver generic or unstructured programs.

Any learning program you invest in must be targeted at, structured for and delivered by skilled facilitators to optimise success. Taking steps to ensure maximum transfer of learning on the job is fundamental. To guarantee a strong return on your investment, engage advisers, trainers, facilitators and coaches who:

- adopt an approach aligned with your organisation's culture

- are likely to influence your people in the kinds of ways you want them to

- communicate messages that are consistent with your organisation's priorities

- are knowledgeable and experienced in their stated area of expertise

- have strong facilitation skills

- inspire people to want to learn and grow — to become a better version of themselves.

Selecting training programs

Working with people to identify the best training programs for them is vital. The people on your team are much more likely to engage fully and derive real benefit from training if they understand why the program is valuable and can contribute to their ability to do their job well. This idea is supported by Malcolm S. Knowles, an adult learning theorist, who in his book *The Adult Learner: A neglected species* suggests that 'adults are motivated to devote energy to learn something to the extent they perceive that it will help them perform tasks or deal with problems that they confront in their life situations'.

Finding the best training program takes more than focusing on a broad competency area. For example, if you are looking for ways to develop someone's ability to be more persuasive when dealing with key stakeholders, considering all communications skills training programs is unlikely to yield a good result. There are many such training programs on the market, but only some of them will focus on the skills of persuasion and influence.

The first step is to look for programs that describe learning outcomes aligned with those you are looking to achieve. If you can't get the information you need from either a training brochure or an organisation's website, take the time to talk to a facilitator of the program. Explore both the content and delivery approach. Be realistic in your expectations; sending someone on a course alone is unlikely to enable them to master the capability. Understand exactly what you are hoping to achieve; for example, will the training program build or improve awareness or teach a specific skill that can then be readily applied? Appreciate what other actions or initiatives you will need to take or implement to achieve the learning outcome.

When choosing the best course to meet your training needs, look for:

- clearly stated learning outcomes and structured curriculum

- relevant and practical content that is easily applied to real workplace scenarios

- opportunities to put theory into practice — a good training program builds in frequent exercises.

To ensure you choose the best organisation to meet your training needs, check that they are able to provide facilitators with the attributes described earlier. To the extent that they are relevant to meeting your particular needs, also consider the following questions:

- Does the organisation have training program development and delivery expertise?

- Does it have a proven track record with a strong reputation? (Ask for references.)

- Does the program offer the flexibility to customise content, format and presentation style to best fit your needs?

- Is the provider knowledgeable about your industry and the implications for the application of the theory.

- Is the program likely to be cost competitive, relative to the value delivered?

Successful coaching programs

Coaching can be an extremely effective development solution if applied well. With the right provider engaged, coaching can be a powerful way of helping people to achieve goals related to performance and personal satisfaction or effectiveness.

Common benefits to candidates of successful coaching programs include improved:

- communication and engagement skills
- robustness and ability to cope with stress
- awareness of their approach and performance
- professional relationships with their manager, peers and staff
- decision making and ability to take prompt action to deal with issues
- self-assurance and leadership strength.

Business coaches can have a significant influence on the people they work with. For example, it's not uncommon to observe coaching relationships that strongly influence major life decisions people make. Regardless of whether career counselling or life success is on the agenda, people frequently explore issues outside the realm of business with their coach. They may discuss quitting their job to pursue a long-held secret ambition, or even a marriage break-up, with a coach they trust and respect.

Essential drivers of a successful coaching program are:

- rapport, trust and respect between coach and candidate
- candidate choice in the selection of the coach
- clear and measurable learning objectives that are agreed, monitored and measured
- skills of the coach to facilitate learning effectively
- appropriate level of confidentiality maintained between coach and participant
- management support and engagement
- participant engagement and commitment
- ability to tailor program content to individual needs.

Further education

By further education I mean academic or professional qualifications beyond those required for entry into a role or profession. For example, an undergraduate degree in accounting may be required for a role, while undertaking further study can build on specialist knowledge or more complex application of principles. In many instances, your involvement in determining the course and study mode your team members elect will be limited to how it affects their eligibility for academic assistance, including financial support, and flexibility to attend school. If you have a close working relationship with your team you may also be able to influence their perceptions of, and commitment to, further education as well as the courses they consider and sign up for.

Sometimes further education is a necessary and valuable development solution. It's not the answer for everything, however. For example, undertaking an MBA undoubtedly has the potential to improve the depth and breadth of general management capabilities. However, it is not the best option if the learning objective is to improve a manager's ability to respond effectively to the day-to-day demands of leading their team. To guide staff to make the best decision regarding further education, ensure the following:

- There is clear alignment between the capabilities the course will develop and the learning objectives.

- Your team member has a sincere desire to study and is willing to see the program through to successful completion.

- That the best delivery mode is elected for each individual. For example, undertaking the course by distance learning may be the most practical option for someone working full time. On the other hand, attendance at group or practical sessions increases some people's ability to learn.

- That a long-term view is taken of the value academic and professional qualifications can offer. It may not be needed now, but how will it assist your team member to develop in their career over time?

- That consideration is given to the quality of the program and the credentials of the institution.

Experiential learning

Put simply, an experiential learning strategy is all about providing people with the opportunity to 'learn by doing'. The more experience you give people and practice they get along the way, the more you are able to influence their development. When managed well, experience really can be the greatest teacher. Look for big and small opportunities to allow people to put theory into practice and learn from experience. Keep in mind, however, the advice of American educational theorist David A. Kolb, who suggests that useful knowledge is gained when the participant is:

- willing to be actively involved in the experience
- able to reflect on the experience
- able to use analytical skills to conceptualise the experience
- able to use decision making and problem-solving skills to apply the ideas learned.

There are lots of ways you can enable people to get hands-on experience. Examples include:

- secondments to other teams and positions
- participation in projects (such as process review or development, or systems implementation)
- working as a champion for change
- job sharing with colleagues
- shadowing or observing a more experienced member of the team
- facilitating or attending meetings

- participating in discussions

- stepping up into higher duties when a more senior team member is away

- taking on responsibility for resolving a particular problem.

To influence value gained from learning through experience, you should:

- be creative and proactively look for experiences your team will benefit from

- promote well—set people up to succeed with opportunities they are ready to take on

- let people fail from time to time—failure can be a powerful teacher of not only what not to do next time, but also what they can and should have done instead

- enable mastery of capabilities by providing opportunities for regular practice.

Self-learning

Self-learning is a vital component of a learning culture and essentially entails an individual guiding their own development. Self-learners identify their own development goals, seeking out the insights or information they need, taking in and comprehending information, reflecting and applying knowledge—all without the instruction of another person. While not always the case, often self-learning also involves personal reflection aimed at developing greater self-awareness. There are many ways a manager can encourage self-learning, starting with creating a workplace culture where taking ownership of your own development is valued and expected.

Ways members of your team can learn for themselves include:

- reading (books, articles, professional journals, blogs)

- observing peers and colleagues with the capabilities they are looking to develop

- seeking feedback that enables greater personal awareness

- mindful observation of themselves in action and consideration of the behaviours they need to bring

- personal reflection and development of strategies for applying new or changed approaches.

Chapter summary: the most important things to do and avoid

Must-do checklist

The most important things you must do to develop the capabilities needed to enable success, now and into the future, include:

✓ grow your own: adopt a planned and long-term approach to growing the capabilities of the people on your team

✓ regularly review capability needs and development plans to maintain alignment with business objectives and priorities

✓ begin development planning by identifying the organisation's, team's and role's core objectives

✓ understand the context within which objectives must be achieved, including obstacles, challenges and complexities

✓ identify the critical competencies needed to achieve core objectives in the relevant context

✓ assess current capabilities relative to those needed; identify development priorities

✓ establish and execute plans with discipline to close competency gaps

✓ build and enable a continuous learning culture.

(continued)

Chapter summary (cont'd)

Common mistakes to avoid

Among the most common mistakes I observe people managers make that undermine their ability to drive learning and development effectively are:

✘ taking too narrow a view of potential development solutions; a training course isn't always the best answer

✘ focusing on 'nice-to-have' development initiatives rather than building 'must-have' capabilities

✘ reflecting on development needs only once a year at appraisal time

✘ limiting focus to technical competence; consider also organisational, emotional, cognitive and interpersonal development needs.

Chapter 8

Reward and recognition

In the arena of human life the honors and rewards fall to those who show their good qualities in action.

Aristotle, Greek philosopher

The performance of most people at work is influenced by the extent to which they feel acknowledged and appreciated. While we are all different, most of us are more likely to work hard and be loyal to an employer who makes us feel appreciated and fairly compensated for our contribution. In this chapter we will explore how to ensure every member of your team is appropriately rewarded and recognised for both their behaviours and their achievements. Important priorities we will look at include:

- the role of acknowledgement and appreciation

- understanding what to reward and recognise

- how to ensure optimal impact of the rewards and recognition you give

- looking for opportunities to praise and why it matters

- linking reward and recognition to performance management.

An organisation's strategic approach to setting salary levels, structuring bonus schemes and aligning pay with performance is beyond the scope of this chapter. Rather, here we will focus on the things a people manager must to do well to leverage reward and recognition efforts.

While the terms are often used interchangeably, there is in fact a clear distinction between reward and recognition. Reward includes any benefit that has a monetary value such as salary, retirement fund contributions, incentives or bonus programs. As we will explore in later sections, rewards don't need to be costly to be valued by the people who receive them. Recognition, on the other hand, includes expressions of acknowledgement, appreciation, due credit and thanks.

Rewarding and recognising people for the role they play is fundamental to motivating effort and inspiring them to stay. While your team are financially rewarded to turn up and contribute to an acceptable standard, getting the best from them typically takes more than paying their salary. We will examine why setting salaries at competitive levels is just the first step to ensuring people feel well rewarded and recognised.

What success looks like

Managers who effectively reward and recognise their staff are more likely to be able to tap into discretionary effort and the full potential of their team. Key indicators that the approach being adopted is effective include the:

- strength of the team's spirit fuelled by a sense of achievement and pride

- results achieved because people are motivated to perform at their best

- belief people hold that they are both valued and respected

- confidence people have in their own abilities and those of their colleagues

- desire people have to stay with the business for the long term

- passion and sense of personal ownership people feel for the outcomes they achieve

- respect and appreciation people feel towards their manager and the organisation.

Managers who are skilled at rewarding and recognising their team's contributions:

- are fair and consistent in their approach to appraising performance

- proactively look for opportunities to acknowledge a job well done

- are disciplined in maintaining high standards in what they reward or recognise

- make behaviour matter as much as the outcomes their team achieve

- build mutual trust and respect into their relationships with their staff

- encourage other people to respect the contributions people make.

Case study
Voice of the people

Among the most successful examples of a formalised rewards program I have observed is that of a large utilities organisation I work with. Greg, the CEO of this business, once described with great pride the approach they take to nominating potential candidates as well as how they select and reward recipients. Throughout the year staff are encouraged to nominate team members they believe should be recognised for either their conduct or their achievements. It is well understood, however, that no matter how impressive their achievements are, only people who consistently demonstrate behaviours in line with the organisation's values are eligible to receive an award.

Rather than simply relying on the willing participation of their staff, a proactive approach is taken to educating their team about why rewarding and recognising one another matters, what it takes to be a recipient of the awards and the types of behaviours people should be looking for in the teammates they choose to nominate. This highly effective strategy has over time helped Greg and his team entrench the program with enthusiastic support from their staff. On average they receive 20 nominations for each of three awards. Not only is the volume exceeding Greg and his team's expectations but the quality of the nominations is consistently high. Staff are actively encouraged to participate and they are expected to approach it seriously. Nominations are accepted only when tangible reasons and evidence of success is provided.

What makes this program particularly successful relative to most I observe is the depth of trust in and respect for the process that has been engendered across the team. The facilitators of the program work hard to maintain buy-in, and the team's eagerness to participate and their respect for the decisions made is a clear indicator of its effectiveness. There was a widely and strongly held view that those recognised and rewarded through the program are consistently worthy recipients.

Key ingredients of their success are clearly evident in the approach taken. Everyone understands they have an opportunity to participate through the nomination process. Consistent and well-understood criteria are applied through the decision-making process. Discipline and focus ensure standards of eligibility are never compromised. The rewards offered are highly valued by the team, and there is room for them to be tailored to the personal wants and needs of individual recipients.

Talking to people involved in the decision-making process provides further insight into why the program works. It is clear that priority is given to selecting people with strong support from their colleagues. In other words, greater value is placed on strongly held views of the team than the perceptions of members of the selection panel. To this point Greg remarked that an individual he has personally nominated a number of times has not yet been recognised. In saying this Greg assured me the right decisions were made — his candidate had not been the best choice and he was proud that his team hadn't allowed his endorsement of the candidate to sway their judgement.

Adopting a strategic approach

The strategic approach adopted and frameworks created at the organisation level are crucial to effective reward and recognition practices. The extent to which a unified and consistent approach is taken across the business depends on the maturity of the strategies, programs and policies in place. Adopting a haphazard and inconsistent approach is one of the most common mistakes I observe organisations make. As we will explore in later sections, the perceived integrity of the approach taken to rewarding and recognising people can have serious implications for trust in the employment relationship.

Strategic priorities of any reward and recognition program should include:

- influencing behaviours that enable success and are ethical

- attracting and retaining qualified and capable people

- motivating people to strive to achieve their full potential

- encouraging people to act in the best interests of the business and its shareholders

- providing an appropriate level of transparency in decision making

- ensuring equity and consistency across the team.

Strategically rewarding and recognising people starts by first establishing what must be accomplished and the standards of performance that are expected. As we explored through chapter 6, we can reasonably expect to hold people accountable only if clear expectations are established.

Staff participation

Encouraging members of your team to get involved in reward and recognition programs is a powerful way to build awareness of, and buy-in to, the standard you are striving to achieve. Asking your staff to nominate peers who demonstrate behaviours or accomplish objectives to a high standard encourages them to focus on and understand:

- the standards of performance that are expected and valued
- how contributions are assessed and appraised
- how seriously achievement of goals is taken
- the discipline of your focus on achieving agreed standards.

Allowing members of your team to contribute to decisions about what and who is rewarded and recognised is a valuable way of encouraging ownership for the team's culture and performance.

The basis of good decisions

Decisions about what and who you reward or recognise are among the most important you make as a people manager. These decisions must be strategic and made with a clear line of sight of the behaviours you want to encourage and those you want to dissuade. It's imperative to remember that this process matters not just to the people you choose to reward or recognise but also to those you decide not to. The decisions you make highlight to everyone what you pay attention to, consider important and value. How you define achievement and successful behaviour is clearly illustrated by the example you make of the people you reward and recognise.

Ensuring your decisions are aligned with and support your culture and performance management objectives is critical to success.

Placing priority on cultural alignment of behaviours, as we explored in chapter 3, is a critical driver of successful culture management. The values expressed through reward and recognition decisions speak loudly; as the old saying goes, 'actions speak louder than words'. It absolutely matters what you say, but it's also true that people gain far more insight into what is really important to you from what you do. It's essential that you, and any managers working for you, demonstrate and encourage desirable attitudes and behaviours through every decision you reach about who to recognise and why.

When contemplating rewarding or recognising someone for a particular action or outcome, consider their overall conduct and impact on the rest of your team. Never hold up as a good example anyone who does not behave in line with your values. To use an example, nominating as 'employee of the month' a top-performing salesperson who consistently behaves badly towards their colleagues sends a poor message. It says financial results matter most, even at the expense of the wellbeing of your team. Don't expect people to separate the results achieved from the poor conduct and be satisfied; most will simply observe a poorly behaving person being rewarded.

Categories of achievement

The standards of performance, capabilities and behaviours people bring to their work should all be considered when rewarding and recognising your team. To make the best decisions, take into account not only the contributions of each individual but also how groups work together to achieve shared objectives. By recognising length of service with your organisation you place a value on loyalty.

Performance

As we explored in the 'Accountability' section of chapter 6 (see p. 139), applying an objective and consistent approach to assessment of contribution is critical. Determining the standards achieved and the appropriate rewards or recognition earned depends on clear expectations of outcomes and behaviours upfront. Without this clarity the ability to align rewards and recognition to real and measureable standards of achievement is undermined.

People managers should be attuned to more than the big, clearly visible achievements of their team members. Yes, it's valuable to recognise the people who kick the winning goals in any competition, but just as essential is recognising those who play the defensive or supportive roles throughout the year, creating openings that enable success. How people perform in their role overall and deliver specific objectives should be reflected by what and who you reward and recognise.

Sometimes it's not the people with the highest profile in your team that have the greatest impact or make the biggest difference. Search for the quiet achievers in your group by looking for their discreet and incremental achievements. Be aware that the nature of some roles will lead to more frequent and easily facilitated recognition of contributions. For example, sales or marketing teams are more likely to be spotlighted because of the role they play in winning new business or coordinating public events. In contrast, the work the finance department has done to ensure the financial security of the business is less likely to be acknowledged, unless of course things go wrong.

It is incumbent upon the managers of all areas of a business to ensure their team receives the credit they deserve. Waiting until the end of the year to recognise progress made in significant projects is a lost opportunity. Stopping to reflect on incremental goals achieved along the way can go a long way to motivating your team to find the energy and keep striving to achieve a challenging objective.

Key elements of performance that should be considered for reward or recognition include:

- achievement of challenging objectives
- superior standards of achievement

- reaching milestone targets

- supporting roles played to enable the success of other team members

- business and team performance.

Capabilities

The capabilities people continue to develop and acquire throughout their employment provide a growing source of potential for organisations to leverage. As someone's capabilities grow, so too does their potential to add value in their role and advance their career with the business. Ongoing development of the capabilities of your people should be encouraged through your reward and recognition efforts.

There are many different ways that a person's capabilities can be rewarded and recognised. For example, focusing on development objectives in performance appraisals will encourage and cultivate a learning culture. Capabilities can be rewarded or recognised through salary practices. Some organisations align salary bands with competency levels, while others reward attainment of qualifications with promotional salary increases. Still others recognise capabilities through position titles. This is an easy way to differentiate levels of competency attained and to recognise personal achievement, but consider carefully the potential impacts on team culture. Adopting an overly hierarchical approach with inflated job titles can undermine the building and maintaining of a respectful and collaborative team culture.

Key elements of professional capabilities to consider for reward or recognition include:

- depth and breadth of knowledge in a chosen profession

- specialist and advanced skills developed

- unique or valuable experience acquired.

Behaviour

As we explored in chapter 3, the development of any team's culture is strongly influenced by the behaviours that are not only expected but also rewarded and recognised. Rewarding discretionary effort, a positive attitude or creative thinking will reinforce and encourage such behaviours. In turn, not rewarding or recognising the contributions of those who drain the spirit of your team, despite their achievements in other areas, sends a strong message about the value placed on acceptable standards of conduct.

If you are serious about creating a healthy workplace culture that inspires commitment and hard work from every member of your team, never reward performance or capabilities in the absence of acceptable behaviours. No matter how clever someone is or how much they get done, if they are not a healthy influence on your team, clients, partners or service providers, their contributions should not be rewarded beyond their base entitlements.

Aspects of behaviour and approach that should be considered for reward and recognition include:

- alignment with the organisation's core values

- integrity and generosity of spirit

- a collaborative and respectful approach

- a positive influence on the spirit of the team

- discretionary effort brought to the role and the business

- commitment demonstrated by effort and time invested.

Service

Tenure alone doesn't add value; retaining high-performing staff is what matters to the long-term performance and sustainability of any business. Assuming that you address substandard performance or mediocre contributions, then you will reward and recognise continuing valuable contributions as reflected by loyalty to, and long tenure with, the business. Service awards should be timed to recognise substantial milestones and provide rewards that reflect the significance of each level of contribution.

It is neither necessary nor advisable to recognise service of less than three years. Most often I observe service awards presented in five-year increments, at 5, 10, 15 and 20 years, and so on. Given the public nature of these types of awards, it can often be difficult to withhold them in the event behaviour expectations are not consistently achieved. It is more appropriate to deal with such concerns separately to afford the individual the sensitivity and confidentiality they deserve.

Types of reward

At the organisation level it is crucial to create a clear strategy and philosophy to guide a consistent and effective approach to rewarding and recognising staff. An organisation's remuneration and benefits philosophy, strategy and policies help managers to effectively manage their staff's expectations and satisfaction with the rewards they receive. Establishing these tools, while outside of the scope of this chapter, is a priority for any organisation.

Remuneration

When it comes to money, everyone is different. Whether we feel underpaid, merely adequately compensated or well paid will vary greatly from person to person. How we feel about what we earn and whether or not it is enough will be influenced by factors such as love of our job, awareness of our market value, desire to serve, financial circumstances, upbringing and personal values. An employer should always base remuneration decisions on solid grounds. A consistent and well-considered approach is most likely to sustain people's perceptions of the fairness and validity of the process and outcomes.

While accepting that each of us is different, I consistently observe the following general truths about people in relation to their income:

- When people are paid what they perceive to be a fair and reasonable salary or wage, the issue of compensation becomes a neutral one. What is far more significant is the extent to which people feel acknowledged and appreciated.

- When people believe their income is below what is appropriate, they are often unhappy and uninspired to perform. Many people are unlikely in these circumstances to work hard or contribute more than they have to.

- If people feel ripped off or cheated, their pay becomes a seriously demotivating factor in their work life. This produces, at best, half-hearted contributions and, at worst, destructive behaviour or departure from the business.

- Paying people a salary well in excess of market value is unlikely to inspire them to strive to excel. Of course some people will respond by making an extra effort; however, more money alone rarely gets the best from people. The financial cost of paying 'top dollar' is rarely repaid by the benefits gained.

- There are some things in life that money simply can't buy, including an energised spirit. Money alone will not compensate for those factors that drain people's energy.

For most people what matters is that they believe they receive a fair income comparable with what they could reasonably expect to earn doing a similar job in another organisation. While there are certainly exceptions to the rule, most people are not inspired to 'go the extra mile' or give more than they have to simply because they are paid above market rates. Elevate someone's pay level and they soon come to believe they are paid only what they are worth, and little to no credit is given to the employer for the pay rise. In the 20–plus years I have worked in management and HR roles I have never once heard someone say they are paid more than they should be.

Wage and salary rises are a valuable way of maintaining competitiveness. For most organisations, however, the extent to which salary can be used to recognise superior contributions is limited by affordability. It is critical to the viability of any organisation that salary levels are kept in line with business objectives and financial limitations. You should never allow people to believe they have automatic entitlement to an increased salary unless it is included in their employment contract or agreement.

It is often not the actual wage or salary but how much they are paid compared with others that concerns people. While some organisations ask and even expect their staff not to discuss their salaries with one another, inevitably some people do. It is common for challenges to arise because members of a team compare salaries, including what they receive as a pay rise. This presents a significant challenge for employers that can only be tackled by applying a fair and consistent process that is well understood. Your team members need to understand:

- it can be misleading to compare the cash component alone; a more accurate comparison would take into account the whole remuneration package, which may reflect hours worked, shift time and length, and travel, for example

- the eligibility criteria for receiving an increase

- how market comparison of salaries is taken into account

- how experience and performance are reflected

- the affordability to the business of providing increased salaries.

Incentive schemes

A 'pay for performance' approach is one designed to provide a total remuneration package that includes elements of both fixed pay and performance-based or 'at-risk' incentives. The proportion of an employee's total remuneration that is at risk typically increases with seniority and the individual's ability to affect the performance of the company. The level of accountability and influence of a particular role will play a key role in determining the size of incentive payment that can be earned.

Incentive plans are a valuable tool for organisations wanting to reward and recognise members of their team for striving for excellence and achieving superior standards of performance. When managed well they provide a valuable opportunity to discriminate on the basis of performance when determining total remuneration outcomes.

Successful management of any incentive program requires that you do the following:

- Set clear and measurable objectives against which performance is assessed.

- Ensure common understanding of the formula that will be applied to calculate incentive payments.

- Make incentives payable on the basis of both achieving defined performance hurdles and meeting expectations of behavioural alignment with the organisation's values.

- Adopt a disciplined and consistent approach to determining payment outcomes. Being lax in the application of incentive plan rules can grossly undermine the credibility and value of the program. In other words, making incentive payments to those who have not successfully jumped over all agreed hurdles undermines the integrity and value of the program.

Benefits

Benefits are various non-wage forms of compensation that offer some financial advantage to employees, but typically at a lower cost to employers. The range of benefits provided varies widely, with some focused on quality of life and others aimed at creating financial advantage through group buying discounts. Examples include:

- subsidised professional services such as financial planning, childcare or housekeeping

- membership of professional organisations and subscriptions to journals

- employer-paid or -subsidised housing

- heath and wellbeing programs, including gym memberships or exercise classes

- group insurance, including health, dental, life, disability and income protection

- higher education tuition fee reimbursement

- additional annual leave days (paid and non-paid).

While these types of benefits can be highly valued, so too can token gestures in recognition of performance and contribution. Within the limits of the budgets available to you, consider providing your staff with impromptu rewards that demonstrate appreciation of a job well done. Examples include:

- movie tickets

- gift vouchers

- hotel stays

- lunch or other meal allowances

- leisure activities, potentially on work time

- shortened work days.

Recognition

Financial rewards play an important role and some people are undoubtedly motivated by money, but it's the appreciation people receive that is likely to have the greatest influence on engagement and retention of the most talented staff. What the vast majority of people care about most is feeling respected, appreciated, valued and acknowledged by their manager and employer.

The person from whom we specifically need acknowledgement depends on our role in the organisation and our character or nature. For example, some people are satisfied if their direct manager acknowledges their work, but for others it matters that more senior managers are aware of their contribution. Such acknowledgement can play a significant part in their feelings of validation or affirmation that they are progressing towards their goals.

Appreciation is about receiving recognition of and gratitude for the quality, value, significance or magnitude of our contributions. My team and I work with people at all stages of their career who commonly report feeling undervalued. It doesn't matter how big their bonus payments are, if their boss consistently fails to thank them when they go beyond the call of duty they are disappointed. Organisations spend fortunes on generous salaries and benefits, yet this investment yields at best ordinary returns because people don't feel appreciated. Some are quick to offer hefty salary packages to attract top people to their team yet fail to do something as fundamental as showing gratitude for their contributions.

Credit is about having our actions, abilities and qualities appropriately attributed to us. Giving credit where it is due is a fundamental principle of successful relationships, including at work. To build trusting relationships that lead to greater dedication and commitment, it's critical that people believe they will be given the credit they deserve once the job is done. Even the most highly paid executive is unlikely to appreciate their employer taking credit for their hard work or achievements. Burned by that experience, they are unlikely the next time around to invest time or energy beyond the minimum required.

Most people will soon begin to distrust their manager's motives if they consistently fail to give them credit, and they may not be the only ones affected. Others who witness this behaviour are also likely to have their perceptions of the manager or the organisation influenced by how they see their colleagues treated.

Optimising impact

To optimise the value of your reward and recognition efforts, your approach must be sincere, considered and focused on the values, behaviours and outcomes you want to encourage. The positive effect of the rewards and recognition you provide on the spirit and engagement of your team depends on a number of key factors including the:

- extent to which the recipient values the reward or form of recognition

- consistency of your approach

- sincerity of your appreciation

- perceived accuracy, credibility and fairness of your decisions

- competitive value of the benefits you provide

- timeliness of your delivery.

Priority 1: value

The extent to which the reward or recognition is valued by the recipient determines the impact it will have. Many award programs provide standardised approaches, but personal meaning can increase the effectiveness of your efforts substantially. Personalising the gift or approach can go a long way to influencing the team member's perceptions of the thought and effort you have invested into recognising them and their achievements.

For example, one organisation I have worked with provides a three-year service award in the form of a book. It's a standard form of reward but it also provides the opportunity for the gift to be personalised. Managers personally select a book they believe is aligned with their team member's personal interests. Another provides managers with a selection of rewards to choose from and encourages them to choose one most suited to their team member. Yet another takes a similar approach but allows the individual to select their own reward.

Priority 2: consistency

A major influencer of the success of your reward and recognition practices is the consistency of your approach. Being consistent in your appraisal and appreciation of one team member compared with another matters; just as crucial is how consistent your approach is with those of other leaders across your organisation. Any perceived favouritism or inequity in the way recipients or gifts are determined is fatal to the credibility and therefore the positive impact of your efforts. Criteria and outcomes must be applied equitably and uniformly to ensure perceptions of consistency.

Priority 3: sincerity

Maximising the value of rewards and recognition requires that both recipients and observers believe they are given with sincere and genuine appreciation of the contributions made. Sincerity demands that you are able to express with conviction the tangible difference the individual or group has made. Conveying honest and heartfelt sentiment is far more likely to inspire commitment and encourage similar behaviour in the future than insincere expressions of gratitude.

A lack of sincerity can be observed in leaders who have little real understanding of the specific achievements they are rewarding or recognising. I have observed cringeworthy examples of leaders struggling even to remember someone's name let alone why they are the deserving recipient of an award. A manager's remote, uninformed commendation does nothing to express sincerity and articulate truthfully why an individual's contribution or achievements are valued and appreciated.

Priority 4: credibility, accuracy and fairness

The credibility of your reward and recognition efforts is profoundly influenced by the extent to which people believe your decisions are fair and accurate. Every member of your team needs to believe that the people who are rewarded are those most deserving of the recognition they receive. Perceived barriers to a fair and equitable process can dramatically undermine confidence and therefore the positive impact of your reward and recognition initiatives.

A common mistake I see managers make is rewarding or recognising staff based on their reputation in the absence of tangible proof or examples of performance. When these team members are perceived by their colleagues to contribute less than their reputations suggest, rewarding or recognising their efforts can grossly undermine trust in your processes.

People need to have confidence that reward decisions are based on relevant criteria that accurately reflect real contributions made. In other words, reward decisions should be credible and transparent, clearly reflected by the criteria and process for determining outcomes. Transparency in your decision-making process will help people appreciate that outcomes are considered, just, objective and unbiased.

Priority 5: timing and setting

The timing of when you reward and recognise people influences your ability to maximise the benefit of your message. Firstly, for anyone to fully appreciate why a specific effort is valued, it's important they are able to recall clearly what they did! The closer to the time of the event that you reward or recognise, the more likely they are to be able to connect the two and understand what has driven their success. Take the opportunity to express appreciation and give positive reinforcement of success 'in the moment', even if a more formal reward is presented at a later date. Waiting for a later opportunity can dilute the clarity and strength of your message.

It's also worth considering the forum in which you choose to reward and recognise people. For example, some people prefer to be acknowledged more discretely than others. I learned early in my career that not everyone enjoys the attention that comes with being rewarded or recognised during an all-staff meeting. While a public forum provides a valuable opportunity to reinforce the importance of the contribution in everyone's minds, a more private setting may have a greater impact on the individual receiving the reward.

Chapter summary: the most important things to do and avoid

Must-do checklist

The most important things you must do to leverage your reward and recognition efforts effectively are:

✓ focus on influencing your team's spirit through a strong sense of personal value and self-belief

✓ demonstrate a generous spirit and proactively look for things that people do well and have achieved

✓ build confidence by recognising capabilities and achievements

✓ be accurate, fair and consistent in your approach to appraising contributions and reaching decisions

✓ build loyalty by recognising commitment through tenure

✓ be disciplined and maintain high standards in what you reward or recognise

✓ reward and recognise only those whose behaviours are culturally aligned

✓ look for opportunities to encourage desirable behaviours and reinforce your cultural values

✓ encourage other people to respect the contributions their colleagues make to collective success

✓ demonstrate sincerity and genuine appreciation.

Common mistakes to avoid

Among the most common reward and recognition mistakes made by managers that you should avoid are:

✘ allowing a distorted view of reality to influence the decisions you make about who and what to reward or recognise

✘ adopting a poorly considered approach that undermines credibility and leads to perceptions of inequitable or unethical practices

✘ failing to recognise significant contributions made

✘ recognising some key contributors but forgetting to include others

✘ adopting an approach that lacks balance and leads to people being rewarded for one aspect of their performance when others fall below acceptable standards.

Chapter 9

Driving change

If you do not change direction, you may end up where you are heading.

Lao Tzu, philosopher of ancient China, author of the *Tao Te Ching*

Among the most common and significant challenges facing managers today is responding to the constant need for change. Our world is evolving, it would seem, at an ever-increasing pace. Smart organisations understand the need to adapt to remain relevant and competitive in a rapidly changing landscape. It isn't difficult to see the rate of change around us. Just look at the world through the eyes of children today and how different it is compared with when you were growing up.

In this chapter we will explore how to successfully lead people through transformational change. We will look at:

- the core competencies and behaviours needed by people managers responsible for driving change
- the importance of trust to the success of any change effort
- understanding the impacts of change on people and how to effectively engage stakeholders
- the role culture plays and how to ensure it enables success
- how to manage the most common obstacles to success.

If recent history is a good measure of what to expect in the future, it's safe to assume many businesses will experience more change in the next three years than they did in the past five. With change a certain part of our future, it's essential that people managers understand how to engage and lead their team to new destinations and ways of working. Innovation of products and services, and reviews of work processes, cost structures, communication protocols and work environments are some of many examples of change most managers need to lead.

Essentially, change management entails the approach taken to shift or transition individuals, teams and organisations from a current state to a desired future state. As a process aimed at helping people to accept and embrace changes in their work environment, it is critical to the long-term viability and success of any business. The primary objectives of any change effort are to maximise the realisation of benefits and minimise adverse consequences or distractions for the team. When managed poorly, change can have devastating consequences not only for performance but also for the spirit and commitment of people. Few things in business have as much potential to undermine trust, erode respect and damage relationships as badly managed change does.

What success looks like

The success of any change initiative is reflected in the extent to which the intended changes have been implemented and embedded. Key indicators of success include that:

- desired changes have been implemented to the standard intended
- changes are integrated into the standard mode of operating for the business or team

(continued)

What success looks like (cont'd)

- your team's spirit is strong and people are enthusiastically engaged in the 'new world'

- people have benefited through the process by gaining knowledge, skill or experience

- undesirable consequences of change have been avoided.

Important indicators of a successful change management approach and process include the following:

- A compelling vision for the future is created and communicated.

- People are aware of and understand the need for change.

- Current reality, relative to the desired future state, is recognised and understood.

- Plans articulate the scope of change, goals to be achieved and strategies implemented.

- Communication is a key priority and managed well throughout.

- Members of the team actively participate in and support the change.

- People have the knowledge and skills they need to change.

- Champions of change are identified and effectively leveraged.

- Progress is monitored and steps taken to overcome obstacles, challenges or risks along the way.

- Change is reinforced to ensure it is maintained.

Case study
Leading out of the dark

Of all the change agents I have met and worked with over the years, none has impressed me more than Pete. While no doubt there are ways in which even Pete can improve, what makes him a great leader of change is his ability to earn the trust and respect of the people he works with. The first time I worked with him he was responsible for driving an aggressive program of change that everyone knew would result in significant job losses. Pete was appointed to head the project team because senior management recognised he had the knowledge, skill and compassion to lead the team through what was going to be an extremely difficult time.

The first thing Pete did was spend time getting to know the people he would be working with. Pete dedicated the first few weeks to learning about not only the people on the project team but also those most likely to be affected. Pete spent hours in conversations with people across the business learning about how they perceived and felt about the change that lay ahead. He made it a priority to personally spend time with people and leveraged insights provided by team leaders. Pete spent a lot of time throughout the life of the change project exploring how people were thinking, feeling and therefore likely to be behaving.

The primary driver of change was the need to dramatically reduce operating expenses. This organisation had experienced a rapid decline in revenue largely as a result of depressed economic conditions and needed to respond swiftly to protect the viability of the business. But while it was widely known that the project would result in job losses, for many months no-one knew which jobs were being targeted, the likely timing and indeed how many positions would be lost. Given this business-wide uncertainty, Pete and his leadership team set about providing as much clarity as was possible at the beginning and throughout the project.

Communication was a constant priority, and every week Pete and his managers met to discuss what the team needed or wanted to know as well as what they were in a position to share or disclose. The approach they took was to be brutally honest, with love; in other words, they were frank yet sensitive. Pete and other leaders provided updates and listened to the team at regularly scheduled forums throughout the process. Core to their success was the empathetic tone of their communications and their willingness to respond openly to even the most challenging questions from the team.

Rigorous planning and disciplined execution of their plans were key to their success. Regular monitoring of progress and adapting plans to respond to shifting priorities or challenges were core components of the way the project was led. Pete never allowed busy schedules and demanding workloads to undermine the discipline they had in place to get things done. For example, scheduled meetings went ahead regardless of who was available to attend, and people were held accountable for delivering information or reports when they had agreed to.

Above all, Pete inspired commitment by sharing a compelling vision of the future. While for some that future meant they would no longer be with the business, he instilled a sense of pride that they were part of making something important happen. Pete helped people to understand that the way they were operating was not sustainable and would ultimately lead to the demise of the business if left unaddressed. While some people did ultimately lose their jobs, there was very little staff turnover during the project and the vast majority left with their self-esteem and confidence in the future intact.

Adopting a strategic approach

Organisations don't change, people do. No matter the scale or complexity of change, success ultimately lies with individuals doing things differently. Driving change effectively requires a focus not only on the big picture but also on how to support each affected person to transition to new ways of working. The absence of this individual perspective is among the most common reasons change strategies either only partially achieve intended objectives or fail altogether. No matter how well you design a process, innovate a product or improve a service, unless the people responsible for putting your designs into action do what they need to, the benefit can't be realised. Bringing people with you through the process and ensuring they have the commitment and capabilities necessary to deliver are primary objectives of any change management effort.

Driving transformational change puts a spotlight on leadership effectiveness. It demands that leaders invest time and energy, make difficult decisions, and demonstrate courage and confidence. The influence a leader has on their team culture, engagement, communication, role clarity, capabilities and ultimately performance is fundamental to successful change management. These priorities don't simply happen on their own; each takes a planned and considered approach with clearly defined goals and strategies for making them happen.

Change planning

Adopting a planned and considered approach to leading change is fundamental to success. Each of the planning principles outlined in chapter 2 applies equally to managing a change process. The person in charge has a vital role to play in establishing a clear vision for the team's future and the strategic plans to turn that vision into reality. The team manager doesn't need to have all the answers but they do need the ability to guide the development of an effective change plan.

While plans are important they add little to no value if not effectively executed. Despite the vast sums of money and energy invested in creating change plans, many are never implemented fully. Some managers allow day-to-day operational demands to limit progress; others lose sight of the plans they established, reverting to a reactive and unstructured approach. Working as a change adviser I regularly observe and experience the challenges of getting managers to move past talking about change to actually making it happen. The best plans in the world will do nothing to drive change unless implemented with discipline and focus.

Creating a compelling vision

A compelling vision is one that makes sense to people and inspires them to want to be a part of it. For change to work, the people driving as well as inputting need to know why it's necessary, why it will make a difference and ultimately why it's worth the effort. You need to be clear not only about what you want to change, but also about your motivations for wanting to make it change. Helping people to understand the drivers and benefits of change is critical to enabling their willingness to engage. When things get hard or people experience periods of change fatigue, knowing why they are following this path will give them a sense of purpose and the energy to keep striving. A compelling vision is one that calls people to action because it offers an inspiring view of the future.

Establishing strategy and goals

Once you have a clear view of what you want to change you need to work out how to get there. Identifying measurable change objectives as well as team and individual goals will help you to target the specific outcomes you want to achieve. Goals and objectives are essential tools for focusing people's energy and talents on the priorities that matter most throughout the change process.

Both short- and long-term goals play a valuable role, particularly when the nature of change is transformational. Incremental changes allow for natural points at which the team gets to stop and observe the fruits of their labour. When driving change over an extended period of time, setting smaller goals the team can celebrate along the way will help to keep the team's spirit energised.

The change plan structure

Outlined here are the most important elements of a change plan:

1 *Drivers of change:*

- What are the primary reasons behind why the changes are being made?

- What problem will be overcome, or opportunity created or leveraged?

2 *Scope of change:*

- What specifically will change? What's in and what's out of scope?

3 *Communication plan:*

- key messages — benefits of and reasons for the change, including what it means for the team and business

- messages targeted to individuals, teams or stakeholder groups

- ongoing communications strategies, priorities, forums and initiatives

- communication schedule — relating to the 'rollout' of specific changes

  - key messages

  - timing and location

  - messengers and support people

  - delivery mode (for example, face to face or email).

4 *Team impact analysis:*

- ways in which both individuals and groups will be affected by the changes

- refer to the 'Driving change' section of this chapter (see p. 210) for further insight into the types of impacts that should be considered.

5 *Risk and resistance analysis and plan:*

- key risks or areas of resistance that may substantially influence success

- strategies to overcome resistance and mitigate risks identified.

6 *Roles and responsibilities of key stakeholders:*

- level of participation and ownership of the change process

- expected approach to leading change.

7 *Implementation plan:*

- descriptions of specific changes to occur

- individual sensitivities that must be taken into account

- timing of implementation stages including deadlines.

Leading change

A people manager's willingness to take ownership for the successful implementation of change is critical to success. Unless managers assume responsibility for actively driving change, the likelihood of achieving change objectives is greatly diminished. All members of the management team, from the senior manager sponsoring the change through to team supervisors, must be unified in their support and consistent in their approach. Lack of unity in the management group dilutes clarity, undermines buy-in and has the potential to heighten already elevated levels of uncertainty, fear or frustration.

Successful change depends on every leader in the chain of command choosing to:

- be visible and demonstrate engagement and support

- lead by example

- focus the team on what needs to be achieved

- demonstrate determination, courage and confidence

- follow through and implement with discipline.

Core competencies

To drive transformational change requires specific leadership capabilities. Ineffective leadership is a common reason for many struggling or failed change initiatives. Failing to communicate effectively, anticipate and manage impacts of change or develop the capabilities needed for the team to succeed are among the shortcomings I most frequently observe in the approaches taken by managers responsible for driving change.

In many ways managing change calls for the same leadership capabilities that enable achievement of any strategic objective. However, dealing with the unique priorities and challenges of leading people through change takes specialist knowledge, skills and experience. For example, identifying the depth and breadth of the consequences of change, or predicting emotional reactions and behaviours, takes a level of empathy and interpersonal engagement skills that many people managers need to develop.

The essential capabilities every people manager needs to drive change successfully are defined by the priorities detailed in the next section of this chapter. In summary, people managers responsible for change need to be able to:

- build trust and earn respect
- establish, implement and monitor progress of strategic change plans
- identify, understand and manage the impacts of change
- assign clearly defined roles to each member of the team
- engage stakeholders
- manage progress
- achieve culture change objectives
- build and leverage capabilities
- manage performance and behaviour
- coach people through change, including the ability to identify and overcome resistance.

Trust: the foundation of success

Trust is fundamental to the successful application of all the tools in the people manager's toolkit, including leading people through transformational change. For most people, to choose to follow you into unknown places or through uncertain times they must first trust in your ability to guide them well. Some managers attempt to demand compliance, but the trust people have in their leader will profoundly influence the choices they make. Each member of your team must have confidence in your judgement, the honesty of your approach and your sincere desire to implement change for the right reasons.

Trust underpins your ability to engage stakeholders to achieve momentum and overcome resistance. Some people, for one reason or another, don't enjoy or are apathetic towards change. Some will take any opportunity to avoid change and a few will resist it unless given compelling reason to do otherwise. Regardless of the reasons for people's hesitancy, inspiring them to change depends on the trust they have in you.

Driving change

Making change happen takes dedicated and focused effort from everyone involved. Driving the process requires managers to proactively work with and influence people, monitor and manage progress, develop the capabilities needed and influence a culture that will enable success. In this section we will explore these and other critical priorities that form the foundations of the people manager's role in driving change.

Priority 1: understand the impacts of change

Before you can begin to plan how best to implement change you need to understand the real and potential impacts or implications for teams and individuals. Before taking steps to make change happen it's crucial that time is invested in thoroughly exploring and assessing impacts, including their likelihood and magnitude. While not all effects are negative, change is likely to have undesirable consequences for some people. These outcomes may not always be avoidable, but the way you approach change can go a long way towards minimising the disadvantage or emotional upset people experience. Consider and plan for implications relating to:

- *culture*—shifted behavioural expectations and how some people will respond
- *position*—for example, role redundancy, changed terms of employment or demotion
- *responsibility*—change of responsibilities and areas of accountability within roles
- *capability*—new or enhanced skills and knowledge required
- *leadership*—change of reporting lines
- *relationships*—new and changed interdependencies and interactions
- *daily work*—impact on daily work routines and priorities.

Any one of these change impacts can lead to adverse consequences for members of your team depending on how they perceive them. Be careful about how you judge the severity or magnitude of these consequences. What may seem to you a small change to someone's role could have far-reaching implications in their mind, fundamentally shifting how they perceive the authority, autonomy, influence, benefits or career prospects associated with their job.

For example, a simple change of reporting line can be perceived as a backward step in the careers of some people. Having to work more closely with another department can fundamentally change how someone feels about coming to work, let alone doing their job. New behavioural expectations could feel stifling and far removed from the workplace culture people have come to know and enjoy. The need to learn new skills could be a daunting challenge that some people simply aren't willing to take on. And so the list goes on. The ways in which people respond to change are varied and at times complex. To make an accurate assessment of change impacts, it's imperative that you know the people you are dealing with. The greater your insight into a person's values, hopes, desires and fears, the more accurately you will be able to predict how they will respond to change.

Priority 2: assign clearly defined roles

Like any other achievement in business, successful change depends on each person on the team understanding and playing their role. Defining and communicating the active roles you need some people to play will allow you not only to focus their energy and efforts but also to target your communication and engagement strategies. Detailed in the following sections are the major roles that are typically played through periods of change. While not all will be formally assigned, it is important to understand who is associated with each and the influence that has on the approach you need to take to leading or working with each person.

Owner

The owner of change is the person ultimately responsible for the successful implementation of change initiatives—where the buck stops. The CEO, proprietor or board chairman are the most common examples of the owners of organisation-wide change. Divisional managers are the most common owners of changes implemented at a department or team level. At times the owner also plays the more hands-on role of driver or advocate. For example, while the owner may not develop and drive change planning, as an advocate they play an active role in winning support and removing roadblocks.

Driver

As the role title suggests, drivers are responsible for driving the process and making change happen. Mandated to assume a direct, hands-on role, drivers lead both the planning and the implementation of change at an individual, team or organisational level. There can be more than one driver of change in a project team, ranging from the managers and supervisors responsible for employees affected by change to specialist change consultants assuming a leadership role in a larger-scale initiative. People can assume the driving role for a particular area of focus or project or for the entire change initiative. Achieving the entirety of the change objectives typically requires that a lead driver of the process be appointed.

Advocate

Advocates facilitate the change process through the support or encouragement they offer as well as their ability to influence other people. Executives and senior leaders who charter and authorise change, often referred to as change sponsors, typically play an advocacy role. A change champion is another advocacy role assumed by people not always in a leadership role. These people are invited to or voluntarily assume a level of responsibility for encouraging and promoting change. They bring energy and share their ideas and experiences with others, enabling transformation to occur in individuals and the group.

Active participant

Active participants include those directly affected by the change and are required to change aspects of what they do or how they do it. These are 'front-line' employees who ultimately bring the change to life through special efforts during stages of change or after implementation when change is operationalised. People working on project teams that are responsible for implementing change are also active participants. Project and change managers, HR consultants and training specialists working to enable change are all examples of active participants in the change process.

Willing participant

Willing participants may be asked to provide assistance in the change process. Typically they are only marginally affected by the change and have little personal investment in seeing the change succeed. This makes this group of stakeholders especially challenging to engage, particularly in cultural environments lacking a spirit of cooperation or focus on 'one team'. For example, the ability to redesign a process in one department may rely on information being provided by another. Similarly, small changes may need to be made to one team's processes to accommodate those intended in another area of the business.

Understanding observer

Observers are not directly affected; however, it matters that they are aware of and understand the need for change. For example, internal customers of a particular team will have an interest in the approach or solutions being implemented. In the event of potential drops in standards of service delivery during the time of change, it will be especially important to engage these people and win their ongoing understanding and support. Another example to reflect on is those members of teams who are not personally affected by job losses even while their colleagues are. To positively influence the spirit and behaviours of these people, it is essential they understand the change drivers and feel confident of the integrity of the approach taken.

Priority 3: engage key stakeholders

Vital objectives of engaging with stakeholders are to persuade and influence their buy-in and support of change efforts. The strategies you need to deploy will be influenced by the extent to which each person is involved or impacted, but influencing their understanding, earning their backing and negotiating their contributions or cooperation are significant priorities. The stakeholders you are most likely to need to engage include those who assume the roles described in priority 2. In many instances key stakeholders are likely to include:

- members of your team — those affected directly and those working alongside them

- people in other teams who need either to contribute to or to work with the changes implemented

- leaders who make or contribute to decisions about financial and other resources you need

- anyone in a position to influence the successful implementation of change.

Among the fundamental priorities on your stakeholder engagement to-do list is to communicate well. The approach you take when communicating with individuals or groups of stakeholders will unquestionably influence the buy-in and support you earn. Poor communication is a common challenge and a key contributor to the failure of many change initiatives. Each of the communication principles explored in chapter 5 is crucial to the success of your change management efforts; this chapter would therefore be incomplete without pointing to the most important elements and how they relate specifically to change.

The core objectives of communicating during times of change are the following:

☑ Influence awareness and understanding by:

   ☑ ensuring people are kept up to date with change priorities and progress

   ☑ keeping everyone appropriately informed about changes that affect them

   ☑ Answering questions and rebuffing false rumours.

☑ Leverage your team by:

   ☑ accessing their knowledge, ideas, perceptions and insights

   ☑ optimising the quality of decisions reached

   ☑ enhancing your understanding of change management priorities.

(continued)

☑ Retain and engage staff, encouraging them to:

   ☑ actively participate in driving change

   ☑ see value in and support change

   ☑ have hope and confidence in the future.

☑ Reward and recognise contributions.

☑ Positively influence the culture of your team.

For most people times of change can be stressful and insufficient information, insight or opportunity to contribute can cause unnecessary anxiety and concern. The process of change can disturb even the strongest person, team or organisation. Never underestimate your team's thirst for information and desire to be kept abreast of your thinking, let alone your actions. Even when you don't have all the information you need to share, focus on building trust that you will communicate what you can when you can. As we explored earlier, trust is the foundation of any successful relationship, and this principle applies equally to leaders of change and the people they ask to follow them.

Understanding the purpose of your communication, what you need to convey, the best timing and frequency, and the medium or forum that will provide the greatest impact are all critical to success. So too is the style you adopt; essential attributes include:

- *authenticity*—be real, upfront and open

- *honesty*—face reality, avoid spin, be open while being appropriately discreet

- *fairness*—give a well-considered, balanced perspective, listen and show genuine consideration

- *compassion*—understand sensitivities, show empathy and act with kindness.

Critical elements of effective delivery of your communications include:

- regularly planning to keep information on target, relevant and timely

- maximising face-to-face communications

- leveraging multiple communication channels to deliver and reinforce key messages

- focusing on the power of daily dialogue between supervisors and members of their team.

Priority 4: manage progress

With change often comes a myriad of tasks and challenges demanding your attention. Progress relies on your ability to establish priorities that focus efforts on the things that have the greatest influence on success. It is essential to disregard or defer inconsequential activities in your change process. Set aside activities that do not add value, and direct your time, energy and resources towards those activities that will give you traction and value. For example, beware of the pitfalls of 'paralysis by analysis'. Collect and assess the data you need but balance this with getting things done.

Establishing milestones and time frames is a central element of goal setting that will play a significant role in keeping you on track. Day-to-day workload demands can often make investing the time and energy needed difficult, so maintaining the discipline of monitoring progress through measures of achievement is a valuable way of ensuring you are on track. Knowing where you are at any given point along the journey enables you to adjust your effort or approach if needed. Holding everyone accountable for reaching milestone and time frame targets goes some way to creating the momentum needed to keep things moving.

Priority 5: ensure culture enables change

For some businesses the biggest challenge they face is shifting their culture to enable change to happen. Teams that are apathetic, risk averse or overly conservative, for example, are unlikely to readily support efforts to implement new and innovative ways of doing things. Transformational change can be hard to achieve unless the way people typically behave includes challenging conventional wisdom and existing ways of working, striving to succeed and giving things a go.

The challenges of driving the culture change needed should not be underestimated. Success requires strong leadership, starting with setting an example of the behaviours needed. Those that matter most will depend on what you are working to achieve. Identifying and setting behavioural expectations and holding people accountable are critical to your success. Discipline and remedial action may be appropriate in some circumstances, but positive reinforcement can be just as effective. Each of the priorities examined in chapter 3 offers insight into the steps you should take to create the culture needed to support change.

Priority 6: build and leverage capabilities

More often than not change brings with it the need to develop or acquire new and improved capabilities. Changes to systems, processes, policies, products and services all have potential implications for the knowledge, skills and experience needed from your team. Identifying specific development needs and solutions is a critical priority through most change processes. Wherever possible set out with a clear view of the impacts of changes on the capabilities required. Assess the extent to which they are already available and, if not, how and when you need to ensure they are in place.

In some cases you will be in a position to develop capabilities over time while others will need to be established before you can fully implement the change. For example, introducing a new technology system to be used by client service staff will require that all 'end users' achieve a level of proficiency or competence by the time the system is launched. In contrast, the capabilities needed to expand your product or service offering to new markets may be developed over a longer period of time. Reflect on each of the priorities and learning methods detailed in chapter 7 and create the plans needed to guide learning.

Priority 7: accountability

Accountability is an essential element of effective change management. It is crucial that you remain sensitive to how people feel and work to influence their engagement, but it is also necessary that you let them know what is expected and where the non-negotiable boundaries lie. For instance, some aspects of change simply won't be open for debate. While people can feel disappointed and even fearful of the consequences that lie ahead, resistance is futile. Equally, it is impossible to satisfy the wants, needs or preferences of every person affected by change. Decisions need to be made and once they are it is reasonable to expect people to cooperate.

For example, as illustrated by the case study included in this chapter (see p. 203), change may be driven by the need to drastically improve the viability of a business due to tough economic conditions. Some people may prefer current ways of working, yet unless efficiency gains are realised it is possible no-one on the team will have a job. Managing change through these conditions often demands tough love. It is imperative that you maintain compassion for the anxiety people feel, work hard to build and maintain hope, but set very clear expectations and hold people accountable for their conduct and contribution.

Priority 8: manage obstacles to success

Many obstacles and challenges can arise along the way to obstruct the progress of change initiatives. Following is a brief description of those that I have commonly observed have the greatest impact. Each can and should be addressed in your change plan; understanding how you will confront and tackle each of them if they arise is a key influencer of success.

Lack of support

Inadequate time, resources and information are all obstacles to successfully implementing change that must be proactively managed. Unless you have the backing you need to access necessary levels of support, these challenges can be difficult to overcome. Having a clearly nominated sponsor with the ability to influence the support provided is critical. Identify what you need and engage the support of your sponsor early in the change process to avoid unnecessary delays to progress.

Sustainability of change

In the early stages of change implementation it is common for progress to be reversed or unwound. It is natural for people to revert to ways of working that are familiar and comfortable, particularly when they are working under pressure. Consider your efforts a success only after a reasonable period of time has elapsed and the changes are still in place. Monitor the changes you have implemented to ensure they continue to be followed until they become an entrenched way of working.

Resistance

Fear and disagreement are the two primary reasons people resist change. Fear of the unknown, of failing or of leaving their comfort zone are common. Fear of losing something they value is also an issue for many people facing change. Perceived loss of job security, status, power, autonomy, authority, flexibility, challenge, career opportunity and quality of work are all examples of losses of value that some people may be concerned about. Disagreeing with the need for change, or the direction or approaches being taken, also causes people to push back and obstruct progress. False beliefs and misunderstandings about what the change will bring can also lead people to resist.

The ways in which people choose to resist change vary dramatically. Some will protest actively and visibly or take material steps to hinder progress. Others will engage in passive resistance and be more covert in their opposition. People can resist on their own or work to build coalitions of people who oppose change. Attitudes will also vary. Some will protest aggressively; others will maintain a more composed demeanour while disagreeing just as firmly with the change. Equally, some people will act constructively and yet persistently to propose alternative options, while others will deliberately and destructively sabotage your efforts.

Regardless of the cause or form of resistance you encounter, your most powerful strategies for dealing with it include developing understanding and trust. Your leadership style and approach, along with that of every other leader in the group, is critical; so too is educating people and encouraging their active participation throughout the process. Coaching individuals and providing them with the emotional support they need can make a big difference. In some circumstances it will be possible and appropriate to negotiate agreements. At times this may include reaching compromises that don't undermine the objectives of change. Your ability to effectively persuade and influence people is critical to managing and overcoming most forms of resistance.

Key staff turnover

Feelings of insecurity during periods of significant organisational change can lead to higher staff turnover. If the future is particularly uncertain, top performers may be tempted to look for new opportunities outside of your team or organisation. While it isn't possible to avoid all staff turnover, the approach you take to leading change will unquestionably influence the stability of your team. All unplanned turnover is undesirable, but it is essential to identify team members who are critical to success, either of the change or of your team more broadly, and apply targeted retention strategies.

Chapter summary: the most important things to do and avoid

Must-do checklist

A consistent approach by all leaders aimed at creating sustainable change is critical to success. Key attributes of the approach that will underpin success include:

✓ develop and implement well-considered and effective change plans

✓ respond and adapt to shifting priorities and challenges as they arise

✓ take steps to mitigate potential risks and adverse impacts

✓ focus on the outcome: monitor and measure success

✓ consult, involve and inform relevant people

✓ be visibly committed to change

✓ only make promises you can keep, and then keep them

✓ communicate effectively

✓ understand and respond to the unique needs and challenges of your team members.

Common mistakes to avoid

The most common mistakes I observe in the approach taken to managing change include:

✗ diving straight into implementation of change without adequate planning and preparation

✗ underestimating the impacts and corresponding responses to change

✗ failing to communicate effectively

✗ failing to adequately define the scope of change

✗ making change optional

✗ focusing on the process alone without consideration of people

✗ failing to develop or acquire the capabilities necessary

✗ failing to engage the team through their active participation

✗ delegating to outsiders

✗ not following through and failing to take accountability for results.

Chapter 10

Leveraging HR

A house divided against itself cannot stand.

Abraham Lincoln, 16th President of the United States

Included in the people manager's toolkit of many organisations are the capabilities of specialist human resources (HR) professionals. When the talents and approach of people on the HR team are well aligned with the organisation's needs, HR can prove to be an invaluable asset in the manager's toolkit. Not only can an effective HR team help people managers to work through complex challenges and sensitive issues, but they can also work with them to achieve longer term strategic objectives. Developing or hiring talent, shifting culture, managing change and negotiating agreements are just a few examples of the ways HR can and often do support managers to build and lead their teams successfully.

In this chapter we will explore:

- the role of HR and how they are able to influence business results

- a formula for successful partnering relationships between HR and business leaders

- inherent challenges of the HR role and how they influence services delivered

- the professional capabilities and services that can reasonably be expected of HR.

Despite the substantial investment businesses make in having HR resources available, often they are either underutilised or somewhat, or even entirely, ineffective. Many of the leaders I work with either fail to or deliberately avoid engaging the support of their HR colleagues. This includes CEOs and business owners who struggle to effectively manage the standard of contribution made by their HR teams. Through development and targeted application of strategies, programs, policies and processes, HR can make a significant contribution to the success of any organisation, but only if leveraged well.

No doubt the HR profession could do more to demonstrate how they add value and earn their seat at the executive table. HR leaders often struggle to demonstrate with hard evidence how their team influences business performance. However, it is also true to say that over recent decades management research and literature has provided ample evidence of the influence of well-executed HR strategies on team and business success. There is no shortage of research to demonstrate that sound and aligned HR practices help organisations improve their performance. There is no longer any excuse for people managers to question the relevance of HR strategy and practice; it is reasonable, however, to challenge the effectiveness of HR teams.

For HR to be the valuable asset it has the potential to be, HR and people managers need to share accountability for success. It isn't good enough for HR to make vague claims of making a difference others can't see, just as it isn't good enough for managers to work around HR people, systems or policies and behave like mavericks. Both parties have an important role to play to ensure HR strategies and the expertise of HR specialists is effectively applied to realise tangible benefits for the organisation. As in any relationship, at the heart of success is trust and respect; sadly, as we will explore in the 'HR's difficult reality' section of this chapter (see p. 236), trust and respect between HR and the business is often lacking.

As you read this chapter consider it in the context of your own relationship to HR. What I will share here is aimed at giving you, as a people manager, insight into the role of HR and what constitutes a successful approach or otherwise. I will also suggest how you can influence the success and value of your working relationship with your HR colleagues. If you are responsible for HR staff, reflect on which if any of the strengths and weaknesses apply to how HR is approached in your business. If you are a CEO or business owner, reflect on the extent to which you are enabling HR to be a valuable tool through the standards you set, the mandate you give and the resources you invest. If you yourself are an HR professional, think about the extent to which these ideas are relevant to you or your team. Reflect also on the relationships you have with people managers at all levels of your organisation and the extent to which they can be described as successful.

What success looks like

HR effectiveness is not just about how well HR teams perform but also about how well the business performs in developing and utilising the potential of their people. When HR are leveraged effectively the benefit to business performance is very real and clearly evident. Sustainability, profitability, productivity, innovation, growth, business process maturity and quality are all business indicators of a successful approach to getting the best from people at work. Successful HR strategy and practice are reflected in each of the measures included in the 'What success looks like' sections throughout this book. Without unnecessarily repeating what I have already shared, I will hit the highlights of the most significant indicators of successful HR:

- Employee satisfaction is high and turnover low.

- People develop careers with the business and stay for the long term.

- Performance levels are high, with few concerns about sub-optimal contributions.

- The culture supports high standards of achievement and ethical conduct.

- Potential employees want to join the team and actively seek out opportunities to do so.

- The organisation meets its legal and statutory compliance obligations with zero claims of inappropriate conduct.

Indicators of a successful partnership between people managers and HR are reflected in the ways each chooses to behave. People managers who value and leverage their relationship with HR:

- believe HR is a valuable resource and their ally

- proactively seek out advice from HR when working through complex people-related issues

- include HR staff on project teams requiring people management expertise

- make decisions influenced by the advice of their HR colleagues

- invite HR to join committees or leadership teams.

(continued)

> ## What success looks like (cont'd)
>
> Core capabilities that HR people need to build successful relationships and make a valued contribution to the business are detailed later in this chapter. As we will explore, to earn the trust and respect of their business colleagues HR must focus on business results and take a pragmatic approach to setting priorities, creating programs, systems or policies, and advising managers.

Case study
Willing partners

While undertaking an HR audit for a professional services business with offices in numerous locations I had the pleasure of observing an impressive example of a partnership between an HR team and their business colleagues. Not far into our process the strength of HR's role in one particular region stood out as a driving force behind many of the results that business unit was achieving. The northern region team reported few challenges recruiting talented staff or retaining them compared with other areas. Annual employee engagement survey results were stronger than any other team and people in the region were often nominated for company-wide recognition awards. Not only were the people results in this region strong but the year my colleague and I met them they had also experienced the highest rate of revenue growth and profitability of any team in the country.

The northern region HR team's almost idealistic description of their relationship with the business seemed too good to be true. Frankly, we wondered the extent to which they were in denial or simply trying to influence our perceptions. Not typically cynical people, we both felt the story being told could have been read from a textbook. We were looking forward to hearing 'the other side of the story' during our meetings with executives and team managers from the region later in the week.

It was a pleasure to discover how very wrong we had been; without exception the HR managers were highly regarded and valued by their clients. Not only did all people managers receive immense benefits from working with HR, but staff we spoke to also gave positive reports about the integral role their HR colleagues played in the day-to-day operations of their business unit. HR managers were reportedly working alongside their clients to participate in a broad range of business initiatives and projects. They were considered strategic advisers and critical partners, there to support the managers to optimise the team's success.

Delving further into the approach to HR in this region it soon became clear why they were successful. Most notable was the strength of mutual trust between the managers and their HR colleagues. The roles and responsibilities of each were clearly defined and respected by both parties; in many instances they shared accountability for outcomes with no signs of conflict or even difficulty. Lines of communication were open, with most managers reporting that they interacted with their HR partner on a daily basis. When implementing business-wide initiatives managers appreciated the flexible and pragmatic approach their HR partners reportedly took to adapting to their needs.

Interestingly managers reported that their HR partners experienced strong resistance and objection from head office HR leaders, who believed all programs, systems and policies should be uniformly applied and complied with. The lack of client focus, commercial acumen or even flexibility of HR managers in the head office stood in stark contrast to the approach of their northern region colleagues. It was clearly evident that the success experienced in the northern region reflected the HR team's commitment to working in partnership with their business clients.

Adopting a strategic approach

As with all things in business the effectiveness of HR starts at the top of the organisation. Ultimately it is the people in the most senior leadership positions who mandate the role that HR gets to play. For some organisations that means the board of directors; for others, the business owner. A skilled and influential HR leader can shift an organisation's thinking and improve the strength of their team's mandate. However, unless senior leaders fundamentally believe in the importance to business success of HR strategy, and unless they are prepared to invest time, energy and resources into developing, guiding and inspiring their team, HR's contribution will be constrained.

In some organisations HR provide expert support and even leadership for strategic initiatives, yet in many more HR's contribution remains limited to operational priorities. It's common for HR teams to focus predominantly on process coordination and information management, and to some extent risk control. Often missing from the list of HR priorities are organisational challenges such as improving productivity, increasing quality, facilitating mergers and acquisitions, and enabling the organisation to bring new products or services to the market. This reflects both HR's failure to step up and business leaders' failure to recognise the critical role HR can and must play. To be a strategic contributor, HR must lead the organisation to develop the human capabilities and spirit needed to achieve and sustain competitive advantage.

It's extraordinary to me how often HR plans are developed in a vacuum, disconnected from the organisation's strategic objectives and priorities. One senior HR executive once told me he didn't need the input of business leaders in their HR planning process because 'we are the experts in people management and should set the agenda for our department'. While this was an astounding attitude for any professional service provider to adopt, it struck me as reflecting many of the attitudes I encounter. Not everyone is quite so arrogant or self-focused in their views, but too many

HR people fail to understand that their role is to enable business performance by applying HR strategies and practices.

Developing HR plans and operating in isolation from people managers and their teams makes it impossible for HR to target their efforts and make a valuable and valued difference. Equally, by failing to engage HR in their own planning efforts some people managers miss the opportunity to leverage their expertise. Even in cases where members of the HR team are skilled and experienced professionals, some managers who are driven by maintaining control or autonomy in their role avoid engaging with HR.

Not only should HR be knocking on the meeting-room door, but senior business leaders shouldn't allow critical strategic planning exercises or HR-related discussions to occur without appropriately engaging relevant specialists, including HR.

The role of HR

Fundamentally the role of HR is to work in partnership with people managers to build and leverage the human capabilities and spirit needed to achieve the best possible results. It is also HR's role to safeguard the organisation from people-related risk by ensuring that appropriate governance and controls are established and maintained. HR influences success by providing the expertise, systems, policies, programs and coaching needed to enable leaders to be effective.

Various HR roles also focus on providing support designed to influence the success and wellbeing of employees. For example, in some organisations counselling and mediation are central to every HR team member's role, while in others staff are directed to specialist members of the HR team or even external service providers for the support they need. The ways things are done can be determined by deliberate structural design or can vary depending on the capabilities and preferences of each member of an HR team.

HR's role can be broken down into four key elements:

1 *envision and plan:* recommendation and development of strategies to achieve objectives

2 *develop:* leadership capabilities and HR tools, including systems, policies and programs

3 *facilitate:* strategy implementation, management and staff advice, team development and process management

4 *govern and control:* legal and policy compliance, risk management, quality, measurement and reporting.

Priority 1: envision and plan

If the purpose of HR is to optimise team performance, and in turn business results, the vision and strategic HR plan should always be driven by the business's agenda. To add real value and deliver tangible results, HR priorities established by HR and people managers alike should be set with a clear line of site to the business outcomes they are intended to enable. Ultimately the primary measure of a successful HR vision and plan should be achievement of the organisation's strategic business objectives.

The strategic plans HR people develop range from those focused on whole-of-business objectives to those relating to a particular team or individual. The ability of HR teams and professionals to develop the strategies needed varies greatly depending on the particular areas of expertise needed. HR can reasonably be expected to provide or access expert advice and guidance to enable the development of strategic plans across each of the people management tools explored in this book.

Typically HR teams and professionals provide strategic advice relating to how to:

- *structure* the organisation, team and each role

- *resource* the organisation or team with the capabilities and capacity needed

- *retain* staff for the long term, particularly those recognised as key talent

- *grow* the spirit and capabilities of each member of the team and the organisation as a whole

- *engage* with the team through collaborating, sharing and listening

- *change* incrementally and transformationally.

Priority 2: develop

HR plays an essential development role in establishing both strength of leadership capabilities and HR programs, policies and systems included in the people manager's toolkit. More often than not the development role of an HR team is delivered through a blend of internal resources and external specialists engaged to provide support.

There are many ways in which HR teams can be leveraged to support the development of leadership capabilities across a business. The following are those I most commonly observe making a positive difference to the strength of leadership teams. To the extent that their skills and experience allow, HR people should personally deliver or engage specialists to:

- work with leadership teams to identify the core leadership capabilities required now and in the future

- provide tools and the expertise needed to accurately assess the current capabilities of leaders

- make recommendations about learning solutions targeted to the development needs of individuals or groups of managers

- provide direct feedback and coaching (where appropriate) to support the development of individual managers or management teams

- provide targeted feedback in response to direct observations as well as advice while guiding managers to apply HR processes

- formally act in a coaching capacity and work closely with an individual over a period of time to influence the achievement of specific development objectives.

HR are intimately involved in the development of the broad range of tools explored in some depth throughout this book. Either by bringing their own expertise or by engaging external resources, HR are responsible for developing programs, systems and policies aligned with and enabling the organisation's strategic objectives.

Priority 3: facilitate

A bridge between HR theory and practice is built by the role HR plays to facilitate success. Through the advice and information HR provides to managers and staff alike, HR people are able to optimise the quality of decisions made and actions taken. This crucial role has the potential to influence results achieved and the quality of relationships among colleagues. Just as valuable is the ability of some HR people to facilitate discussions or debates to ensure everyone involved adopts a respectful and collaborative approach. Their ability to promote calm and considered discussion can be a crucial enabler of success.

While certainly not always the case, many HR professionals are skilled facilitators of workshops aimed at the development of cohesion and collaboration. Whether focused on developing greater awareness, understanding, cooperation or harmony, HR people can often assume the role of facilitator and guide teams to positive outcomes. HR's capabilities in this area can be particularly useful during challenging times when heightened pressures and sensitivities can make reaching amicable solutions difficult.

Yet another valuable facilitation role HR plays is in coordinating the effective implementation of programs and processes. Take for example a recruitment assignment. Typically a lot of work goes into coordinating various steps and a number of people are involved in the process. Ensuring everyone is kept informed and has the information they need when they need it can itself be a major undertaking. This is also true of processes such as annual performance reviews, where enormous value is gained from HR team members facilitating company-wide communications and record keeping.

Priority 4: *govern and control*

The role HR plays in maintaining appropriate governance and control mechanisms to protect the organisation is vital. While ultimate responsibility rests with the board of directors, CEO or business owner, HR shares accountability for effective corporate governance and legal compliance as they relate to employment standards and practices. The most common risks and compliance obligations HR are expected to influence or manage include:

- to provide a work environment free of bullying, harassment and discriminatory behaviour

- to ensure all staff are kept safe from hazards that threaten their physical safety

- full compliance of all staff with relevant legislation that governs their role.

Acting as custodians of the team's spirit and culture, HR people should lead by example and demonstrate the standards of integrity and conduct expected from every member of the team. Influencing the way people choose to behave is a central concern of HR people working to ensure compliance with standards mandated by law or ethical business practice. HR also often provide training and education to managers and staff aimed at developing their understanding of the compliance obligations mandated by law, industry standards, company policies, individual employment contracts or collective agreements.

HR and people managers should work together to identify key measures of compliance and achievement of quality standards. Once metrics are in place, responsibility for the quality and value of data captured should also be shared. Too often I observe organisations failing to get any real value from HR-prepared and -presented management reports. Typically both play a role by failing to discuss and agree on the information and undertake the analysis needed. Performance metrics support governance and control objectives only if they are targeted and provide insights that enable corrective or improvement actions to be taken.

HR's difficult reality

Let's face it, the brutal truth is HR doesn't have the best of reputations among large sections of the business community. Of course there are those who are recognised for the integral role they play in influencing their organisation's success, but as a general rule confidence in HR is low. All too often I hear managers complain that HR are not on their side and in some cases are working against them. Many believe HR people have their own agenda that has little to do with what the rest of the business is trying to achieve. Scepticism and mistrust are fuelled when HR are vague about their role and contribution; it is very common for people to feel HR has something to hide.

The scope of this chapter doesn't allow for an in-depth analysis of why HR's reputation is what it is. Rather, I will focus on my own observations of the most common reasons HR teams struggle to win confidence and build effective partnerships with business leaders. Later I will share common roles HR people adopt that obstruct them from achieving their own objectives. Before I do, however, let's first take a moment to appreciate the nature of HR's role and the inherent complexities they face in managing their reputation and relationships. Consider, for example, that often HR's ability to provide full disclosure of their work is limited by the need to maintain confidentiality or act with sensitivity. Add to that the need to make judgement calls about the contributions of other people, sometimes more senior than themselves, and already you have two potential obstacles to building and maintaining trust.

Much like an internal audit function, the jobs HR people sometimes need to do can cause others to mistrust and even dislike them. The often highly visible and active role HR play in organisational restructures that lead to job losses is just one example. Even the most reasonable business decisions sometimes have undesirable consequences for people. There are endless examples of issues HR get involved in that are highly sensitive and emotionally charged. While certainly not always the case, responsibility for decisions that affect people's careers and lives can fall unfairly on HR. In other words, HR managers can be seen as the 'bad guys' who make managers do things they don't want to.

Regardless of the personal views HR people hold, they are rarely in a position to stand up and tell everyone what they think. There are lots of things that go on behind closed meeting-room doors that HR can't share. Hiring, counselling, disciplinary and firing decisions are made; discussions are held about the personalities and approaches of people across the business. HR are often privy to sensitive information about senior people, and sometimes they must challenge leaders who lack integrity or compassion. None of these stories can be told and often people are left to form their own perceptions, which are often not flattering of HR. It can be a lonely job in HR when your colleagues are sceptical or distrustful of you but you can't put up a defence.

HR people can find themselves in difficult positions and the harsh reality is that without the trust and respect of managers and staff they can't do their job. By definition it's impossible to act as a trusted adviser if people don't trust you, and it's difficult to effectively coach or persuade people to adopt a particular point of view if they don't respect you and the way you go about things. Unless HR people are able to build and maintain trust, irrespective of the innate complexities of their role, they are effectively useless to their organisation. Following are the approaches I most often observe HR people adopt that hamper their ability to build effective relationships with people managers and make a substantial contribution to their team's success.

HR puff and stuff

I believe this is an apt term for those who have an overly idealistic view of HR priorities or practices and lack appropriate focus on business outcomes or commercial realities. These HR people are disproportionately focused on the needs of employees at the expense of business success. The advice provided is often disconnected from the strategic objectives of the organisation with little clarity provided about how recommended approaches will affect business performance. HR puff and stuff people are often known for 'mothering' without adopting an appropriately balanced focus on performance.

Fun police

Often HR come under fire for being too focused on risk controls at the expense of adding value and enabling business results. These HR people are single-mindedly committed to the governance and compliance obligations of the HR function. They are referred to as the fun police largely because of their often dictatorial approach and uncompromising attitude, which many leaders and staff find highly constraining. These HR people are far more inclined to tell people what they can't do rather than telling them how to achieve what they need to within the boundaries of policy, law and ethics.

Program pusher

These HR people are heavily committed to the programs HR roll out—for example, culture change, employee wellness or engagement programs. Such programs have the potential to add enormous value, but these HR people tend to focus on the development of the programs rather than on their effective implementation. Typically they consider success to be reflected in a program's existence rather than in the realisation of benefits and tangible returns on the organisation's investment. The biggest mistake these HR people make is pushing compliance with programs while failing to coach and guide managers to effectively leverage or apply them.

Professional capabilities

As in any other advice-based profession, each HR person's depth of knowledge, skills and experience determines the role they are capable of playing. Often I work with organisations that assign responsibility for HR to people with limited experience or even formal training. Typically these people are capable of performing an administration and process coordination role but are expected also to give advice about issues with potentially serious consequences for individuals and the business. The greatest challenge these HR people face is the absence of a more experienced HR leader to guide and support their development in the role.

Identifying the professional capabilities needed must start with understanding the role the organisation needs and wants performed. The attributes required will vary with the level of accountability and complexity of each role. The specific capabilities needed will also vary depending on the focus and priorities of the particular HR role. For example, not all HR managers are expected to play a hands-on role coaching and developing managers, whereas in some organisations that is a core focus of the job and measure of success.

Following are core capabilities and attributes needed for anyone to work as a strategic HR adviser.

Business knowledge

- Understands the vision and strategic objectives of the organisation.

- Has a well-developed understanding of the organisation's products, services and operational processes.

- Is aware of the competitive landscape and the implications for HR strategies and priorities.

HR strategy

- Is commercially astute and able to align HR strategy to key drivers of business performance.

- Integrates HR practices into unified solutions to business problems.

- Is able to articulate the benefits of HR strategies and win buy-in of business leaders.

- Is able to identify and manage to appropriate priorities.

Organisation development

- Has expert knowledge of approaches to developing the spirit and capabilities of a team, including culture, engagement, retention and learning strategies.

Coaching and facilitation

- Is emotionally intelligent and able to remain objective.

- Understands how to influence the self-awareness and personal development of other people.

- Is able to persuade and influence the beliefs, ideas, opinions and actions of others.

- Is a skilled mediator and able to negotiate resolution to disagreements and conflicts.

Change

- Understands the key drivers of successful change and is able to lead the organisation's approach.

- Is able to engage key stakeholders in the process of change and overcome resistance.

Risk and compliance

- Has in-depth understanding and awareness of employment law and the organisation's compliance obligations.

- Understands potential risks and is able to establish and implement mitigation strategies.

- Is able to educate and advise managers to ensure lawful and ethical applications of HR policies and processes.

Irrespective of their experience or seniority, successful HR people will be:

- optimistic and engaging

- readily and willingly accessible

- fair, ethical and compassionate

- pragmatic in putting HR theory into practice

- results focused.

Successful partnerships

For any relationship to be successful both parties need to want to make it work and take responsibility for the attitudes and behaviours they bring. While HR must earn the trust and respect of managers, the willingness of managers to be open-minded and receptive to HR's influence matters just as much. For value from the organisation's investment in HR to be fully realised, both HR teams and people managers need to understand the importance of a united and integrated effort. Unless HR recognise there is little point in developing strategies or programs that managers neither support nor implement, they'll fail to engage effectively with the business. Equally, unless people managers understand it makes no sense to go it alone when they have HR colleagues whose support they can enlist, they will fail to leverage the benefits of HR expertise.

A well-developed appreciation of the perspectives and needs of each party is an important starting point to building a solid working relationship. HR needs to understand what people managers want, need and expect of the role HR should play, but also the outcomes people managers want to achieve and the approaches they prefer to take. In turn, people managers need to develop an understanding of their HR colleagues' responsibilities, priorities and objectives. With mutual respect and understanding, HR and people managers will find ways to leverage the value of a true partnership.

Conflicts and challenges arise most often between HR and people managers when:

- their respective roles and responsibilities are not defined, causing a lack of clarity about authority and accountability

- managers favour approaches that HR believe are not aligned with the organisation's values, strategies or policies

- HR favour approaches managers see little value in

- one party lacks trust or confidence in the other.

Most people managers want HR simply to provide advice and tools that will help them to manage their teams and achieve their business goals. Usually they don't especially care about HR best practice; they just want the best results. To enable a successful relationship, HR need to work with their clients to target priorities and tailor approaches to the unique objectives of each team. Even corporate-wide programs can be delivered in ways that are tailored to the particular circumstances and even preferences of a team. Put simply, HR need to own their part in building a successful partnering relationship by delivering high-quality value-adding services.

In turn, managers need to adopt a spirit of cooperation and respect. It is reasonable to expect people managers to be proactive in getting HR involved when needed. For that to work managers need to be trusted to use their judgement and decide when to manage events or make decisions on their own and when to consult with HR. The challenge arises when managers have previously experienced frustrations working with HR and have lost confidence in their advice or contribution. Understandably these managers can be reluctant to engage HR, and their frustrations should be taken seriously by the organisation. However, the managers' concerns should not be allowed to undermine and exclude HR. As in any other area of the business, underperformance concerns should be addressed fairly.

Your opportunity to influence the approach of your HR colleagues by working closely with them should not be underestimated. Working together over time can help you to find appropriate points of compromise or can shift the approach of either party to better accommodate others' needs or preferences. In other words, if at first you struggle to build successful working relationships with your HR colleagues, persist and avoid giving up too prematurely. At least for a reasonable period of time, work to influence their approach. It may well be that by helping them to develop greater understanding or by nurturing greater trust in your relationship, the initial challenges and obstacles to working together can be overcome.

Accessing HR

The priority your organisation places on adopting strategic and expert approaches to people management will have some influence on decisions made about appointing specialist HR staff to the team. It doesn't always make sense to employ people on a permanent or full-time basis, however, especially when the team is small or the HR needs of the business are changing rapidly. More often than not organisations need to prioritise the positions they can afford to fill, and understandably HR doesn't always come out on top of that list.

If HR expertise isn't included in your people manager's toolkit, tap into the information, advice and guidance you need in other ways. While unlikely to replace or fully replicate the value a skilled and aligned HR professional can add to your team, there are lots of different ways you can access HR know-how from external sources. Here are some examples:

- Participate in online discussion forums such as LinkedIn where experienced HR professionals are likely to be interacting.

- Read blogs—not just those written by HR professionals but also the experiences of fellow people managers shared through regular posts.

- Join professional networking groups that meet regularly and provide guest speakers. Many will offer the opportunity to request speakers able to facilitate discussions about particular topics relevant to the group's members.

- Share experiences with industry colleagues; for example, if possible tap into the advice of HR managers working for partner organisations.

- Read books about specific topics and those that share the experiences of accomplished people leaders.

- Subscribe to professional journals that include articles on people leadership.

- Look for mentors who are skilled people leaders and can offer advice and guidance.

- Engage the services of an outsourced HR team, either as needed or retained on a part-time basis.

Chapter summary: the most important things to do and avoid

Must-do checklist

To realise maximum benefit from access to HR expertise in their toolkit, the most important things people managers must do are:

✓ commit to developing close working relationships

✓ interact regularly to enable a united and integrated effort

✓ focus on fostering mutual trust and respect by working with a spirit of cooperation and reasonableness

✓ understand the type of HR role your colleagues are mandated to play and maintain reasonable expectations of their contributions

✓ be open-minded and receptive to the advice and recommendations HR provide

✓ proactively engage the support and input of HR when appropriate.

Common mistakes to avoid

The most common mistakes I observe people managers make that undermine their ability to effectively leverage HR include:

✗ failing to respect the specialist expertise of HR professionals and the value they can add to strategic decision making

✗ disregarding sound advice provided by HR because of an emotional or arrogant attachment to a particular point of view or approach

✗ expecting HR people to deliver results well beyond their level of capability

✗ overlooking or disregarding compliance expectations that your HR colleagues are obligated to enforce

✗ giving HR limited insight to help them understand the business and how to support your team.

Conclusion

Throughout the pages of this book we have explored the things that matter most to getting the best from people at work—not just a compliant contribution or what people give when they feel obligated to, but the very best of their talents and energy. Each of the people management tools we have examined can in one way or another, individually and collectively, help you to build a capable team and influence the strength and vitality of their spirit. By applying what we have explored, not only can you overcome the common challenges faced by people managers, but you can guide your team to achieve great results they may not even perceive as possible.

As you work to leverage the full potential of your team and achieve great results, remember that when talented people are highly motivated and bring the full strength of their knowledge, skills and experience to their role, truly optimal outcomes are possible. It is your job to influence the vitality and enthusiasm of your team by nurturing their spirit. Focus on pumping positive energy into your team's spirit and do everything possible to limit those things that have a draining effect. Focusing on the strength of the positive energy people have in reserve will allow you to tap into their discretionary effort, the stuff people do because they want to.

As you apply the tools in this toolkit, keep in mind that the strength of an individual's spirit will influence the choices they make about how to behave. Consciously or not, each person on your team chooses how they act. A strong spirit leads people to make positive choices about how they conduct themselves. If they have plenty of positive energy in reserve, they are more likely to choose effective ways of behaving. Feeling trusted, respected, appreciated or empowered, for example, will energise your team's spirit. Conversely if they feel unimportant, insecure, bored, confused or resentful they are more likely to be drained of positive energy and to behave in ways that undermine their own and their team's success.

Keep in mind, however, that no matter how well you implement the approaches we have explored you are still likely to encounter people management challenges from time to time. Overcoming them will always take energy and discipline; being a great manager will always demand commitment and strength of spirit from you. You will always need to focus and strive to succeed in the face of the many people-related complexities and obstacles you will inevitably face.

As I sat down to write the conclusion to this book I wanted to share a few more words of wisdom from Richard Branson, someone I find inspiring and believe to be among the greatest people leaders the world of business has seen. As usual I struggled to decide which particular piece of Richard's wisdom I wanted to share so I have included three of my favourites:

To me, business isn't about wearing suits or pleasing stockholders. It's about being true to yourself, your ideas and focusing on the essentials.

Because no one, no one, not even bankers!— leaps out of bed in the morning just to open an envelope or read an email or answer the phone. They get out of bed to make a difference.

Richard Branson, *Screw Business as Usual*

A journey of a thousand miles starts with that first step. If you look ahead to the end, and all the weary miles between, with all the dangers you might face, you might never take that first step. And whatever it is you want to achieve in life, if you don't make the effort, you won't reach your goal. So take that first step. There will be many challenges. You might get knocked back— but in the end you will make it.

Richard Branson, *Screw It, Let's Do It*

Each of these quotes contains a nugget of gold, and collectively they sum up the message I want to leave you with. First, focus on the essentials. No doubt you can learn a great deal from detailed or sophisticated theories and models, but what matters in the end is that you do the essential things that have the greatest impact on human capability and spirit. Each of the approaches and strategies we have explored will contribute to your ability to tap into the full potential of every member of your team. You really don't need to take on an approach that's any more complex than what I have described in this 'back to basics' guidebook.

Second, appreciate that for people to be at their best they must feel they are making a positive difference. Understand the unique nature of each person on your team and help them to feel a strong sense of personal value, to have great relationships and to find purpose and meaning in their work. Help them to believe in the future and their ability to influence it. Often all it takes for people to succeed is to have one person who not only believes in them but is willing to encourage and guide them to achieve their dreams. Be that one person; be the person who inspires others to greatness through your belief, effort and example.

Finally, you need to step fully into your role and work hard to become the best possible manager of people you can be. You must act with courage, face the tough stuff and keep striving no matter how rocky the path or big the challenges you encounter. What matters is that you step up and meet the challenges of your job and strive to reach the heights you and your team are capable of. No matter where you are in your journey to becoming a successful manager of people, whether you are already highly accomplished, on the road to success or just setting out, remember that your ability to influence the success of others starts with the commitment you make and the ownership you take.

Together, your approach and the tools you apply form a web of interacting factors that collectively influence the spirit, capability and performance of your team. Every tool in your toolkit needs to be leveraged as part of a greater whole that will ultimately lead to the success of each person you work with. Work hard to build a compelling vision and strategy that inspires your team. Support everyone to succeed by providing a cultural environment that builds trust and motivates people to want to give their best. Recognise recruitment for the bedrock of your HR strategy that it is. Face it, if you get that part wrong you are making your job hard right from the get-go.

Communicate often and communicate well; understand the need and desire of people to have information and insights that help them do their job and believe in the future. Continue to build your team members' capabilities throughout their careers with you. It doesn't matter if they are progressing up the corporate ladder; what matters is that they continually learn and grow. Set an example for others to follow, and when people get things right and do them well reward and recognise their contributions. Finally accept that change is a constant and ensure you approach it well.

This book is intended to be your guide, a reference tool that points you towards the things that matter most. I urge you to refer again to each section as you need to and, by working to apply each of the checklists provided, to avoid the common mistakes I have observed.

Remember, though, having fun at work isn't only okay—it's necessary!

Index

Learn more with practical advice from our experts

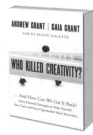